THE

Baby Boomer's
Guide to

the NEW
WORKPLACE

THE
Baby Boomer's Guide to
the NEW
WORKPLACE

RICHARD FEIN

TAYLOR TRADE PUBLISHING
Lanham • New York • Boulder • Toronto • Oxford

Copyright © 2006 by Richard Fein
First Taylor Trade Publishing edition 2006

This Taylor Trade Publishing paperback edition of *The Baby Boomer's Guide to the New Workplace* is an original publication. It is published by arrangement with the author.

Published by Taylor Trade Publishing
An imprint of The Rowman & Littlefield Publishing Group, Inc.
4501 Forbes Boulevard, Suite 200, Lanham, Maryland 20706

Distributed by national book network

Library of Congress Cataloging-in-Publication Data

Fein, Richard, 1946–
    The baby boomer's guide to the new workplace / Richard Fein.— 1st Taylor trade pub. ed.
        p. cm.
    Includes index.
    ISBN-10 1-58979-267-X (pbk. : alk. paper)
    ISBN-13 978-1-58979-267-8
    1. Labor market—United States. 2. Middle-aged persons—Employment—United States. 3. Occupational training—United States. 4. Occupational retraining—United States. 5. Baby boom generation—United States—Economic conditions. 6. Older people—Employment—United States. I. Title.
    HD5724.F375 2006
    658.14—dc22   2005030997

㊾™ The paper used in this publication meets the minimum requirements of American National Standard for Information Sciences—Permanence of Paper for Printed Library Materials, ANSI/NISO Z39.48-1992.

Manufactured in the United States of America.

In honor of my mother, Celia Fein,
who proofread the manuscript at age 92
and made helpful suggestions

Contents

Introduction

THE BABY BOOMER'S *Guide to the New Workplace* is an upbeat, yet realistic, book for people who will work during their senior years. It is a book about the reasons people work, the choices they make, what they enjoy, and what they don't. Therefore, it is also a book about preparing because only those who prepare really have choices. Others have to accept what the Fates ordain for them. *The Baby Boomer's Guide to the New Workplace* is also about knowing how to get what you want because only those who know what to do will achieve what they want.

Not that long ago, a book like this would not have been necessary. Picture yourself anywhere in the United States in the late nineteenth century. A newspaper reporter approaches you and asks what you think about retirement. In all likelihood, you have no idea what the reporter is asking. "I plan to work until the day I die," you might say, "unless I get hurt or something happens and I am unable to work. In that case, I have three sons to support me and a daughter to take care of me." If you had heard about Chancellor Otto von Bismarck's state pension program in Germany in 1881, you would probably say, "Heck, it doesn't start until you are 65 or 70 years old, and most folks will be dead by then anyway."

Fast forward to 1935. The New Deal institutes the Social Security program, in part to get older Americans out of the workforce so that younger people can take their place. People over the age of 65 expect that they will stop working, sit in a rocking chair, and then die.

Move forward in time again to the beginning of the twenty-first century. Some people are retiring at age 57 and playing golf. Others are still working in their 70s, some at their lifelong jobs, others in completely new roles. Some are working because they want to—for social, civic, or spiritual reasons. For others, work is a necessity, and they dread the day they need to get by without a paycheck.

You could picture the changes in retirement options this way:

Grandparents' Time (no real options for most people)
birth > school (maybe) > work (for males) > illness (likely) > death (certainly)

Parents' Time
birth > school (probably at least high school; increasing percentage going to college) > work (perhaps many years with the same employer) > retirement (frequently a company pension plus Social Security).
This generation often saved in life and bequeathed in death.

Now (many options, especially for those who prepare)
birth > education (almost certainly) > work (for most people, including women) > many years of relatively good health when work is optional (possibly) > death (eventually)

The Year 2010 and Beyond
birth > education > work > years of relatively good health > death
Private savings are low, defined-benefit pensions are less common, and the guaranteed income of Social Security is likely to be less generous.

To get a clearer picture of where we are and where we are likely to be in the future, let's look at how things have changed.

Positive Changes

- Fewer jobs entail repetitive tasks, sore muscles, and aching backs. From the perspective of physical capability, a person can do more jobs past the point of peak physical health. Of course, this doesn't apply to all jobs. What's more, the physical ability to do a job is not the only criterion. Energy, temperament, and mental flexibility are also factors.
- Most people have achieved a higher material standard of living than their predecessors. Therefore, the *potential* for saving discretionary income has been greater.
- People are living longer in relatively better health. With life and health, a person can make choices about what to do with their time.
- People tend to change jobs with some frequency in the course of a career. Therefore, they are somewhat adept at looking for jobs and adjusting to new circumstances.
- What to do with retirement is not just a question for men anymore. Since more women are in the workforce, more women have choices to make about retirement. (Of course, retirement should be a joint decision. If you are fortunate enough to have a spouse, make sure that he or she is a part of your planning for retirement.)
- Many people have been able to enjoy a substantial amount of pleasure and recreation as an integral part of their life. Others have deferred some dreams or spiritual missions while raising families. These people are not seeking endless rounds of golf at the end of a working rainbow. Besides, there are still weekends.

Negative Changes

- The underpinning for financial security is shakier. Company pensions are frequently less generous and less secure than in the immediate post-World War II era. Social Security is already weaker through an increase in the age for maximum retirement benefits. The stock market is not the cash machine of the 1990s.

- Material expectations have increased along with material attainment. Therefore, the perception of what is "enough money to get by on" has moved upward.

- The potential for a long life is a two-edged sword. Americans face the risk of exhausting financial resources long before death. When raising a family, you buy life insurance in case you die too young. What do you do in case you live too long?

- Family structures are a bit tenuous, and divorce is frequent. What's more, many adult children do not expect to support aged parents financially. Indeed, sometimes aged parents need to lend support to adult children.

- There is a youth culture. Young is good. Old is, well, old.

What Is in This Book for You?

The choices you have about working in retirement depend significantly on a number of factors, including preparing for the future, knowing your options, and learning how to achieve them. *The Baby Boomer's Guide to the New Workplace* addresses each factor in one or more chapters.

Chapter 1: This chapter will share with you the reasons other Americans over the age of 55 continue to work. The reasons may be cause for inspiration, reflection, or concern, but they are all important for you to consider. Furthermore, I will discuss steps to take so that you will have the best chance to work at a job you want until you decide to leave. I will encourage you to continue developing job skills, name recognition, and a professional network. In addition, I will tell you how to change the work options available to you with your current employer. (Yes, you can really do it!) Financial planning is important, but we will explore that in a later chapter.

Chapter 2: Are you thinking about downshifting a bit with your current employer or trying something completely new? This chapter will tell you about employment options that have worked well for others.

Chapter 3: Many people have found contract employment a good way to make a good living without the traditional long-term tie to a specific employer. This chapter tells you what you need to know.

Chapter 4: Chapter 4 explores franchising. Some older people try franchising as a way to make a living or to fulfill other deferred dreams. This chapter tells you what you need to know if you are considering this option. There is also an extended sidebar on owning your own business.

Chapter 5: Volunteering is a $260 billion industry. Why do people volunteer, and what is it that they do? What should you be asking before accepting a volunteer opportunity?

Chapter 6: Here we cover the job search techniques that work for those over the age of 55 so that you will know how to get what you want.

Chapter 7: This will show you a new approach to your résumé. Since your résumé is most often your ticket to an interview, and getting a job interview is often the hardest part of the job search, you cannot rely on the résumé that's sitting in your desk drawer.

Chapter 8: This chapter will give you tips on writing a cover letter that will not be overlooked.

Chapter 9: Here we will show you how to ace your job interview under new circumstances.

Chapter 10: This chapter discusses life on the job, whether you are the senior kid on a changing block or the new kid on a new block. There are some major myths to debunk. Also, many people work well into their seventies. In fact, approximately 266,000 Americans are working past the *age of 80*! How do they do it and why?

Chapter 11: This chapter will tell you the basic things you need to know to have the best chance at a financially secure future.

The Baby Boomer's Guide to the New Workplace is about having the best available options for working as you get older. It is not a book about social policy, common prejudices, or the state of the American economy. In that context, this is a good place to say a few words about age discrimination.

AGE DISCRIMINATION AND YOUR EMPLOYMENT SECURITY

- The Age Discrimination in Employment Act (ADEA) became law in 1967. It forbids discriminating against a person 40 years of age or older in employment.
- In 2002, almost 20,000 age discrimination claims were filled with the U.S. Equal Employment Opportunity Commission (EEOC). The EEOC determined that there was reasonable cause in only 4.3 percent of the claims. By contrast, over 50 percent were deemed to have no reasonable cause and over 33 percent resulted in administrative closures.
- When older Americans are fired, caught in a Reduction-in-Force, or denied promotional opportunity, they often feel this adverse action was based on age discrimination. When the economy has entered recession periods over

the last 25 years, the number of age discrimination complaints filed goes up. Following the chat rooms populated by people in the over-50 age group also makes it clear that many seniors consider discrimination the villain. Indeed, in a survey conducted by the AARP (*Staying Ahead of the Curve, 2002*), fully two-thirds of respondents between the ages of 45 and 74 believe that age discrimination exists in the workplace. Sixty percent said that older workers are the first to be targeted when there are reductions in force designed to cut costs.

- It is not clear that older Americans suffer more unemployment than younger people. The official unemployment rate for those over the age of 50 in 2002 was about 3.9 percent, significantly lower than the national average. Even so, there may be considerable hidden unemployment. Some people may be involuntarily retired, reluctant consultants who really want a salaried job, seniors working only part-time or at a position far below what they held for years, or so discouraged that they have simply stopped looking.

Any discrimination is abhorrent and un-American and being involuntarily unemployed is a painful situation. I am not a lawyer, but a close look tells us that there are two pragmatic things to consider. *First,* losing a job may be the result of business conditions and the connection with age may simply be that advancing age often correlates with relatively high salaries. For example, assume that John is earning $80,000 a year and producing enough to justify that salary. It makes no business sense for the employer to remove a proven performer simply to bring

(continued)

in a younger person. The employer has nothing to gain and something to lose by doing so. On the other hand, if John is not producing enough to justify his salary, he might be dismissed irrespective of his age. In that case, John is the unfortunate object of a reasonable business decision rather than a victim of age discrimination.

Similarly, if a company reorganizes due to changes in technology, consumer taste, or general market conditions, positions may be eliminated. If a company outsources a function or eliminates a level of management, positions will also be lost. Some people refer to dismissing higher paid employees as 'salary discrimination.' That may well be a social and economic problem, but it is not age discrimination. (*To pursue this point a bit, it is possible that an employer may feel that someone else can do John's job just as well for a lower salary. Without going into all the business risks involved with trading a proven performer for a potential performer, if John loses his job, it is still because of a business decision based on salary, and not discrimination based on age.*)

Also, dozens of studies and business press articles attest to the fact that many companies are deeply concerned about *retaining* their older employees, especially in good economic times.

Second, if John believes that age discrimination was a factor in his loss of employment, he may wish to pursue a remedy through legal action. However, *The Baby Boomer's Guide to the New Workplace* will not offer John legal advice. Instead, this book will tell John the steps he can take to make his job more secure before losing it and what he can do to obtain new employment if that becomes necessary.

Now that we know what is in *The Baby Boomer's Guide to the New Workplace* for you, let's take a closer look at chapter 1 and find out why American seniors work.

Why Do Older Americans Work?

W HAT MOTIVATES people to work when their peers are playing golf every day or just sitting at home? There are many reasons and they vary with the people you ask. However, you will probably recognize yourself in one of these descriptions:

- You started planning for your midlife and senior years about 20 years ago. You wanted to have the option of working at a fulfilling job until *you* decide to stop. Therefore, you have made sure to remain valuable to your employer through productive work and a consistent upgrading of your skills. Through building professional contacts and increasing your professional value, you have also increased the probability of securing a new job should that become necessary. In addition, you have been careful with finances, so you can stop working if you find something better to do.

- Like many older Americans, you have multiple reasons to continue working. For one thing, you like what you are doing. Yes, on some days it would be nice to be outside playing golf, but overall there is a satisfaction in meeting challenges and getting things done. Even if you have been with the same employer for a number of years, times change. The challenges faced a few years ago have given perspective on the current situation but not the solutions. Even old problems require new thinking. In addition, you like most of the people at work. Except on the most hectic day, there is still the water cooler and lunch break. Your work life is a part of your broader social life.

- Of course, there are other possibilities. Perhaps you are developing plans to pursue a dream you deferred for family or financial reasons. When you started working about 30 years ago, you had a very narrow and perhaps overly pragmatic view of what you could do. Deep inside, you want to pursue something else, for example, running your own business. You may be spending weekends taking necessary courses or gaining practical experience in the dream-related pursuit.

- You might be a person who deals with issues only as they arise. Perhaps you are totally absorbed in your current life situation or perhaps you feel that the future will take care of itself. You have not thought about your 50s and 60s all that much, but you anticipate working for the most basic of reasons: you will need the money. You haven't saved very much, and your 401(k), such as it is, won't be enough to live on, even with full Social Security when that kicks in. You are getting by at present but do not know what will happen when you have to stop working.

- Perhaps you are a person who does not have a large income but matches that financial reality with a modest level of material expectations. Maybe your goal as a younger person was to marry and raise a family. After the children have grown up, you still want to make a difference in the world. You may get very involved in a church or civic organization, perhaps one dedicated to helping less fortunate families. These activities replace raising children as a fulfilling experience. Financially, you will get by with a small pension, some savings, and perhaps a spouse's income or life insurance proceeds.

- The pocketbook and the spirit are not the only reasons for working. You may work to give life some structure—so that life does not become daytime TV and crossword puzzles. Perhaps your spouse is still working, and you do not want to be alone all day.

- You may be a person who will no longer need to work because of financial need, personal satisfaction, structure, or any other reason. At some point between the ages of 50 and 65, you will have earned and saved plenty of money. You will have the means to relax and have fun. You look forward to playing golf or traveling, but work is no longer on the radar screen. It is possible that you will tire of so much leisure time after a few years. At that point, you may well seek a part-time job or a volunteer experience.

- Maybe you have accepted an early retirement offer from your downsizing employer. At first, you may have felt lucky to be retiring relatively young. However, before long you may begin to feel unemployed rather than unencumbered. You may be bored and/or have realized that the financial package you received will not keep its purchasing power over the next 25 to 35 years. Even if you do not need to work for emotional reasons, you will need to work for financial ones. People who were planning to retire anyway when they accepted the early retirement package are probably in a different

situation. For them, retirement has simply come a bit earlier than expected and may have included a nice financial
incentive to ease the pain.

- Unfortunately, you may be a person in a difficult situation.
Perhaps you have bounced from one low-paying job to
another, have no real savings, and no pension. You cannot
stop working for financial reasons and when you do work,
you do not earn very much. There is some social life at
work, but essentially every week is simply the continuation
of a struggle to get by. If you have a spouse, he or she may
be too ill to work. You may have found life a struggle until
now and confront a financially precarious future, especially
when you are no longer able to work at all.

To summarize, you may work for personal satisfaction—chasing a
deferred dream, staying socially connected, or doing something of
benefit to humanity. On the purely pragmatic side, you may also
work because you need the money to maintain your material standard of living.

The Baby Boomer's Guide to the New Workplace will show you
how to create the best possible options for yourself as you consider
working after the age of 55. In the next part of this chapter, we will
look at the six things you can do to have the best possible employment options as you get older. I have listed them in the order of
greatest importance to people who are still working. If you have
stopped working and are thinking about working again, start your
reading with Priority #2.

Priority #1: Be in a Position to Keep Your Current Job until You Want to Do Something Else

Remaining valuable to your employer is no small matter. The decision to work is not unilateral. A person has a job only if an employer

wants to employ him or her. For your years of valuable service, you earned a paycheck, not a claim on permanent employment.

There are several things you can do to maintain or increase your value as an employee:

First, ask for growth assignments. Enhanced skills make you more valuable, even if that fact is not immediately reflected on your salary stub.

Second, stay current with developments in your field through professional associations and continuing education.

Third, understand that when the curtain goes up at work, you are paid to produce and not to rest on previously earned laurels. You are likely to have the option of staying with your current employer if you continue to contribute at least as much as your compensation package (salary plus benefits) costs. You may find yourself on the way out if you start to coast after the age of 50.

A helpful hint: do not talk about retirement in public. You can undermine your own security by casual remarks about how you would like to spend more time fishing or traveling around the world. If people have the impression that you are not interested in your working future, you are less likely to be offered new assignments or training that would make you more valuable.

Priority #2: Be in a Strong Position to Get Another Job If You Need To or Simply Want To

Even if your current employer thinks that you are the most valuable employee and hopes that you will work there forever, your job may disappear. In fact, your *entire company* may disappear through merger or business failure. Here are some things that will ease your way to the next employer:

- **Enhance your name recognition in your field:** Speak at events sponsored by your professional association, and write short but informative articles for your professional trade journal. Participate respectfully and thoughtfully in a civilized professional chat room. These efforts are not terribly time-consuming and can even be enjoyable. For future reference, your name recognition will give you easier entrée to recruiters, networking referrals, and other employers. (They will also make your current manager happy when you bring favorable publicity to the attention of relevant outsiders and your manager's boss.)

- **Build your network before you need it:** In job seeking terms, your network is that group of people who may be willing to help you find your next job for personal, professional, or altruistic reasons. It is wise to build your professional network before you ever need it. Build positive relationships with everyone you meet through your job and retain their contact information. This includes present and past coworkers, members of trade and professional associations, customers, and even friendly competitors. Whenever you can do someone a favor without violating professional ethics, do it. The strongest relationships with people are built when you do not need anything from them.

Start to keep records of your professional contacts from all sources. Begin to view those contacts as part of your future, not just an event occurring in the course of a day. Do for others before you need them to do for you.

Priority #3: Prepare for Alternate Employment

Ask yourself this question, "If my employer went out of business completely tomorrow morning, what would I do for a job?" To formulate your answer, you should start considering possibilities.

- **Seek a similar job with a different employer:** Who would those employers be? Start developing a list of potential next employers now. (See chapter 6 for a systematic approach.) Identify ways in which your current job is *not* a perfect match for the next employer. If it is a matter of skill sets, try to develop them on your current job or through appropriate training, even if you have to pay for it yourself. If it is a matter of industry expertise, start reading the applicable trade journals and websites. Of course, some of what you are doing now would be a good match for your next employer.

- **Test the waters in something completely different:** Larry provides an example. Larry had already played trumpet in a band from time to time, but mostly it was just jamming. He began to think seriously about building up a local following for weddings and anniversary parties. This additional income became an alternate income when Larry's regular job was eliminated. The experience of Sheila provides another example. Sheila was considering opening her own card shop. To find out more about the realities of that business, she took a weekend job in a local shop that sold greeting cards and gift items. You may find ways to practice a new skill in a voluntary environment. For example, Jeannine wanted to get involved in event planning. She volunteered to write promotional materials for a local charity and to organize their annual fund drive.

Obviously, you do not want to do anything that jeopardizes your current job. Make sure that you remain fully engaged in what you are paid to do and do nothing that would involve you in a conflict of interests with your current employer.

Priority #4: Make Your Company
More (Older) Worker Friendly

Start encouraging your company to take steps that will help you
(and many others) as you get older.

- **Educate your employer about the benefits of phased retirement:** By whatever name, "phased retirement" is designed to
  let veteran company employees stay with the company, but
  in a reduced role. That might mean reduced hours, fewer
  weeks a year, or less stressful responsibilities. Before
  approaching your employer, be sure to understand the benefits to the company: *First,* phased retirement programs are a
  useful way to attract and retain employees even if most never
  seek to use it. The fact that a company makes an effort at flexibility with its employees says something positive about a
  worker-friendly environment. *Second,* the company retains a
  person's talents. Somebody may want to contribute but opt
  out of the rat race. If they have the talent, the company
  should at least explore the possibility of keeping them in
  some capacity. *Third,* although a phased retirement program
  makes the most business sense when demand for employees
  is high, it makes sense for the company to get started now,
  irrespective of the economic climate. The company wants to
  be prepared (and not just starting from scratch) when the
  economy is booming and good employees are hard to hire.
- **Encourage your employer to support the establishment of
  a corporate alumni association:** Arm yourself with a list of
  benefits so that you can build a constituency for the idea
  among both employees and employers. (See sidebar.)
- **Fight antiage biases:** Many companies, to their credit, sponsor
  workshops for employees to combat racial, religious, cultural,

ENCOURAGING EMPLOYERS

Some employers will be more open to suggestions for the changes discussed here than others. However, here are some things to remember:

- **Know how the employer will benefit:** You have a good chance of success if the employer sees how the change is in the company's enlightened self-interest. Therefore, you need to know the advantages to the employer indicated in this chapter.
- **Check out other companies:** Check the websites of competitors to see if they are already doing what your employer should be doing (e.g., a phased retirement program). You can point to other companies as success stories. Many inhibitions are alleviated when people know that the idea works.
- **Follow your company's protocol:** Even the best idea will go nowhere (and might get you in some hot water) if you do not raise it the right way. First stop should be your immediate manager. Ask him or her what they think about the idea and how you could carry it forward.
- **Anticipate concerns:** A typical concern is *cost*. However, you will not be suggesting something expensive, such as expanded drug coverage under a medical policy. To the contrary, you will be suggesting something that saves your company bundles of cash that would otherwise be spent on recruiting costs or lost to potentially profitable projects that could not be staffed. A second concern is

(continued)

timing. *Why now?* The answer is that retention is going to be a big problem whenever the job market is hot and when baby boomers get older. Since there are lead times involved in instituting changes like phased retirement, it is important to get ready *now*. Otherwise, the company will have to start from scratch when the need to attract and retain employees is more pressing. In addition, the fact of moving on a desirable change *now* sends a positive message to employees *now*.

or gender biases. According to a report of the Conference Board, which disseminates knowledge about management and the marketplace, only about 19 percent of companies include material about age bias. Even in those cases, age bias is usually not the *sole* topic of an antibias workshop. Encourage your company to include age bias as a topic that needs to be addressed. Perhaps the format could be a *Workers across the Generations* workshop that presents the issue as people of different generations working together productively.

Priority #5: Make Your Company More Retiree Friendly

We will speak more about this in the next chapter. For now let's just touch on some essentials. Some companies allow or invite some of their retired employees to return to work, usually on a less than full-time basis. This is not an act of charity. The company benefits in the following ways:

- The retiree has already adopted the company's culture.
- They frequently know the players on the job already.
- Retirees tend to have a good work ethic.

CORPORATE ALUMNI ASSOCIATIONS

Benefits to employees:

- Access to people who have shared common on-the-job, professional experiences
- Supplies potential source of job leads in other companies as most of the alumni now work somewhere else
- Encourages social connectedness, much like a high school or college alumni association

Benefits to the company:

- Contributes to employee-friendly image (no one needs the company's permission to create an alumni association in any event)
- Provides easier access to former employees the company may want to rehire on a long term or on an as-needed basis

One place to learn more about corporate alumni associations is at www.corporatealumni.com.

- They are a good example (and may even act as mentors) for other temporary workers and for younger workers.
- Health insurance expense is already paid for through the retirement program and does not have to be charged to the operating budget.

If your company does not have a program of this type, perhaps you can raise the idea with management. It is important to understand however, that this is *not a no-brainer* for the company. Bringing a program into being requires a lot of work, and the employer must deal with a host of compliance issues just as it would for other employees. Furthermore, the company must make sure that line managers do not encourage employees to "retire" so that they can be hired back as temporary workers.

Also, it is important for you to realize two critical factors: (1) coming back on a part-time or short-term basis is a possibility, but *not a right or a guarantee*; (2) the company may be concerned about your ability to adjust to a less demanding job than you had before.

Priority #6: Be Financially Prepared for a Six-Month Job Search

This means building up your accessible financial reserves and developing an austerity budget. If you have a cushion in your time of need, you will not be pressed into accepting a job just to keep body and soul together.

We will be reading stories about working seniors in *The Baby Boomer's Guide to the New Workplace*. Three of them appear in this chapter. The first is Alan Stein, a person who planned a transition from one career to another. The second is Ray Winter, a 79-year-old, full-time employee at Wal-Mart. The third is Eugene Isenberg, a chairman and CEO of a large corporation.

A Seamless Transition between Careers

Picture yourself as a full colonel in the U.S. Army, specializing in logistics, and contemplating what to do after 26 years of military service. Alan Stein, now 55, was in that situation a few years ago. "I couldn't sit around and do nothing," Alan related. "Besides, my wife, who works part-time as an optometrist, didn't want me hanging around the house and driving her crazy. On top of that, we

SOME THOUGHTS ABOUT WORK AND HEALTH

This is a book about working. Still, there are about 2.6 million Americans between the ages of 51 and 59 who are retired. According to a report from the National Academy on an Aging Society (number 5, February 2001), "Most of them are satisfied with their lives. They enjoy freedom from stress and flexibility in how they spend their time." There are also about 1.8 million workers age 70 and older. Are there some differences in attitude between young retirees and older workers? "Retirees are almost three times more likely than workers to say there is absolutely no chance they will live to be 75 (13 percent vs. 5 percent) . . . The proportion of young retirees who say they are in very good to excellent health is half that of workers." Conversely, "Older workers are more optimistic they will live into their later years than their nonworking counterparts." Among people at least 70 years of age, only 8 percent of the working group think they will have "absolutely no chance" of living another 10 years vs. 24 percent of the nonworkers. When asked a question reflecting certainty about living another 10 years, 17 percent of workers said yes vs. only 10 percent for nonworkers.

have two children at home. If they are to go to college, I had better be going to work. I knew that I wanted to manage something, and I was able to get a good position at CALIBRE because they do work for the military and that is what I know very well."

One of the things Alan likes best about his new career is that he is actually doing some different things with his skills than he did before. For example, he spends a significant amount of time developing courses to train military officers in precommand situations.

In addition, Alan has worked extensively on implementing a commercial supply chain, Enterprise Resource Planning tool, to manage army logistics. "I never thought I'd find myself involved in such a massive software effort. CALIBRE encourages employees to stretch professionally. That sets up a good working environment because it allows for personal growth," Alan told me.

When he joined CALIBRE, Alan found that there was a bit of adjustment to make working with younger colleagues. "They were very bright and hardworking. However, I found that they tended to have shorter-term horizons and were committed to their technical profession more than to a specific company. I think that older folks perhaps put a slightly different value on longevity with a company. Still, it must be said that we older folks are valued for our experience. As long as we don't turn people off by starting every conversation with 'back in my day,' we are generally respected for our contributions and our leadership."

Looking down the road, Alan is interested in doing some teaching or nonprofit community work. "I am thinking about this quite seriously. I will check out those possibilities more intensely before I decide on a next step in my life," Alan indicated.

A Two-Week Retirement, Interrupted by a Ten-Year Love Affair

When you enter the Wal-Mart in Sapulpa, Oklahoma, you will often hear some beautiful music. Not Muzak, but real singing . . . and it's live! Ray Winter, the 79-year-old greeter is a full-time employee who loves to sing. Sometimes it will be a spiritual requested by a customer, like "Amazing Grace" or "How Great Thou Art." At other times, it will be a jingle that Ray has composed himself. For example, here is one, sung to the tune of "Danny Boy":

Wal-Mart will always be my song of praise
For it was Sam that brought us happy shopping days.
I do not know just how Sam has made it so,
He has always had the prices low.
Sam's values will always be the very best.
Wal-Mart will always sell—and sell for less.
How marvelous. Sam's values will always be the best.
Wal-Mart will always sell— will sell for less.

Ray came to Wal-Mart about a decade ago, in January 1994. "I retired at age 65, and that lasted all of two weeks. I was bored and didn't like watching soap operas on TV so I was working for a local supermarket, sacking and carrying out groceries, and I sang to the customers. A friend, who happened to be a Wal-Mart shareholder, suggested that I talk to the manager at the store in Bristow, Oklahoma about a job. The manager asked me what I liked to do, and I said 'Sing. Would that be OK to sing for Wal-Mart?' The manager said great, and I have been singing ever since. After being on the job four months, I was asked to sing some of my jingles at the annual shareholders meeting in Fayetteville, Arkansas. Believe me, that was a thrill."

In his younger days, Ray earned a living by working buildings and grounds and by selling insurance. However, he always liked to sing, albeit not on the job as he does now. Ray sings in his church choir and has volunteered to sing for local prison inmates in McAlester and Taft, Oklahoma. "I even sang with the Platters once," Ray recalled. " I was at one of their performances, and they asked if anyone in the audience wanted to become the sixth Platter for the next number. I am not shy, so there I was singing 'Sixteen Tons' up on the stage. Now when I go to Branson, Missouri, my wife and I go see and hear the Platters for free."

> Why did I choose to include a story about someone who works at Wal-Mart, a controversial company that is admired by many but disdained by many others? The reason is this: it is important to realize that a working situation, which might not be right for some people, is a wonderful opportunity for others.

Ray works the evening shift, generally 3 p.m. to 10 p.m., five days a week. He would prefer the day shift, but people with more seniority have asked for that. Maybe Ray will acquire the additional seniority for a change in shifts. "I plan to stay with Wal-Mart. If I won the lottery, I would probably take a vacation, and then come right back to work. I have made many new friends in the Wal-mart Supercenters. One customer at the store in Tulsa even adopted me as her 'Second Father,' which includes receiving a present from her on my birthday, Father's Day, and Christmas. It took me 50 years of work before I got to Wal-Mart, and I plan to be here for years to come."

Doing Well and Doing Good

Eugene M. Isenberg, age 74, is chairman and chief executive officer of Nabors Industries Ltd., the world's largest provider of land and platform drilling contract services for exploration and development of oil, gas, and geothermal wells.

So why does Gene Isenberg continue to work? "If I preferred to do anything else, I would," Gene told me. "As long as I am healthy and functional, managing a business is what I would like to do."

Gene did retire in a sense, 18 years ago. He sold his company and was certainly set financially. "But I was going bonkers," Gene recalls. "By taking the reins at Nabors Industries, I turned a bankrupt company into a profitable enterprise with a $7 billion market capitalization. For me the motivation is achieving commercial success and other business goals. I also have the chance to contribute significant sums of money to good causes, like the Isenberg School of Management. I am better at doing that than at sitting on committees and such."

If Gene were to advise a friend who was considering retirement, he would ask him or her three key questions (assuming that finances are not an issue):

- How much will you miss your job if you leave it?
- Is your decision reversible? That is, could you return to doing something you enjoy once you leave it?
- What do you want to do that you will find fulfilling? Golf and fishing have a scarcity value. That is, the more you do it, the less it means to you. Think carefully about how you want to use your time. You can use weekends for recreation.

In this chapter, we learned why people work when they might have retired. As we shall see in the next chapter, working and slowing down a bit can sometimes go together.

Phased Retirement: Getting Out Slowly . . . Early Retirement: Moving On Sooner

CCORDING TO A report issued by Watson Wyatt Worldwide (a human resources consulting firm) in 2004, "Nearly two-thirds of full-time workers over the age of 50 hope to scale back their hours or work in a more flexible environment before retiring completely." However, recent studies also indicate that only 16–23 percent of employers offer a program of this type.

A number of potential advantages exist for you in this downshifting of your work life, which is typically referred to as bridge employment, phased retirement, or other company-specific names.

- The transition from a life where work is a dominant component to a less structured life is not as abrupt.
- The job may now focus on those things that you like to do the most (no guarantee, of course).

- Continued employment on a part-time basis can offset the possibility of social isolation.
- Financial needs may be ongoing, although they may be curtailed.

Let's take a look at some examples. The "Casual Retiree Program" at Aerospace Corporation provides a case in point. Aero employees are eligible to retire at age 55. The employee may work up to 1,000 hours per year. The details are up to the arrangement between the casual retiree and his or her manager. Therefore, a person could work one day now and then or for a period of months. Aero started the program in the mid-1980s to address problems with the IRS over employees who retired and then came back as consultants.

A company benefits by retaining institutional memory. Also, it is easier to renew security clearances than to start afresh.

Similarly, Wendy Reitherman, vice president of human resources at Varian Medical Systems, headquartered in Palo Alto, California, considers their company's phased retirement program to be a win-win situation. For the company, there is a chance to transfer knowledge gradually from workers who would like to leave to those who will be taking up related responsibilities. In addition, the program helps retain some employees who might otherwise decide to retire more abruptly from the company. Finally, the program reinforces and enhances the image of the company with other employees and the community. For the employee, there is an opportunity to adjust gradually to a different lifestyle in a supportive and planned way.

The flexible work arrangement could mean two possible changes: the same job, but with a reduced schedule, or a different job with reduced hours. A minimum of 20 hours per week on a three or four day schedule is required. To be eligible, a person must have been a full-time employee for at least five years and be at least

55 years of age. In addition, they must plan to retire from the company within three years. This is not an entitlement program. The company must determine if it is able to accommodate the employee. Varian does make every reasonable effort to do so.

Hanging Up the Spikes? Yes, No, Not Really

Sometimes, plans for a full retirement meet an unexpected change. John Sayles of Muscatine, Iowa, can tell you about that. He formally retired from Stanley Consultants, Inc. as an urban planning consultant on March 28, 2003. Two days later, he was on a plane to Salt Lake City, Utah. John was needed to do some work on a project there. It has been like that ever since. When the company calls, John, who is 70 years old, gets the option of taking a temporary assignment. "I like the work, the people, and the extra money," John remarked.

John is one of 15 to 20 'retired' consultants who still works up to 20 hours a week at Stanley Consultants, Inc. "I still feel very connected," John noted. "I still have my desk, computer, and employee pass key."

The last few years have been a period of transition for John. He cut back to a 32-hour week the year before he retired. "I took Fridays off and loved those three-day weekends," John recalls. "Now that I am working half-time or less on spot assignments, I have more time for household projects and some additional volunteering. The challenge may come in the winter. It sometimes gets bitter cold here, and you don't feel like spending a lot of time outside. I do not anticipate doing this spot work forever. People tend to drift away from that, especially as technology changes, and it becomes harder to keep up."

John has also had some exciting new experiences. He was vacationing in Colorado when he received a call from a company senior vice president. "Would you consider going over to Iraq, John? We are sending a team to do some reconstruction work and could use a good planner." John discussed the request with his family. Before long he was working seven days a week, 12 hours a day in Baghdad. "I was the oldest one on my team, but two of the other fellows were age 65. We worked mostly in the presidential palace in the Green Zone, but sometimes we had to go out into the city. This was my first time commuting to a work site in a Humvee with armed shooters riding along," John recalled. "Even with the security concerns, I am glad to have gone to Iraq. With the eyes of the world watching us, our team was doing something good to help the people there. In a way, the Iraq experience was the cap on my career."

Post-Iraq, John has still been working at Stanley Consultants. His current project is the Heritage Room, a storehouse of information about the company from its origins in 1913 up to the present. "One way to convey the Stanley culture to new employees, clients, and guests, is to let them know about our history," John observed. "I have been with the company since December 1963. I've stayed because of the fine people I have worked with over the years, good company management, the challenging assignments, chances to travel overseas, and Muscatine is a good place to raise a family. If I won $2 million in the lottery today, I would still want to work part-time at Stanley Consultants, Inc. I enjoy the associations with my coworkers, such as dealing with clients, and the assignments keep me challenged."

Downshifting: An Option You Might Earn

Randy Roody worked for New Hampshire-based Teradyne for 18 years, first as a regional sales manager and then as a product manager. He put in 60-hour weeks on a regular basis. "I never left work before 7 p.m. and seldom ate lunch with anyone unless it was a client," Randy told me. On the other hand, Randy had a plan to retire around age 55. "I couldn't live like a king, but my wife and I could live well enough," as he put it.

About a year before his anticipated retirement, Randy notified his boss. Unexpectedly, his boss asked if Randy could continue to work three days a week as a troubleshooter, with the same pay on a prorated basis, and full benefits. "This was great," Randy recalled. "I hadn't intended to take another paying job. However, if I were going to work at all, this would be in a much less stressful work environment, and I would be making more money than by doing anything else I could think of."

When the time came for Randy to transition from full-time (and then some) employee to part-time, he did something he recommends to anyone in that situation: he got away completely for four weeks. "It's very important. In our case, we spent a month in Europe. The point is if you are really away (no e-mails, no phone calls) you can't get pulled back into the job. The company learns how to do without you, and you learn to stop thinking about yourself in the context of your old job," Randy advised.

This new, downshifted work life was very appealing. "I continued to use the expertise I had developed. Just as important, I continued to learn from the new employees. They often introduced me to new computer skills and new ways of thinking. Because I didn't interface with external clients, whatever stress I experienced was self-imposed. I was less in the loop on some issues then I used to be, but for me that was a blessing. It enabled me to focus on getting things done rather than going to meetings." Not one to sit at home, Randy also became a volunteer treasurer for a small non-profit association in his community.

Randy spent five years in his three day a week capacity. (Full disclosure: sometimes it was four days, Randy told me. "Teradyne was also my hobby.") Randy moved to a new cubicle, and Teradyne shared in the cost of a laptop that he used both at home and at work. Physically, he was away from his old account team but was in the same area of the plant. "Initially it was difficult because my marketing boss, who was new, did not really have plans for me, and we improvised for a while. I often went home at 5 p.m. and felt guilty walking out of the plant that early. That may have been one of my most difficult transitions—leaving on time. As the weeks went on, my new boss or others in senior management began to give me projects. At one point I worked collections for a while, which were hung up in documentation issues. At another point I reviewed long lists of obsolete inventory looking for material that might be of value to customers. It was a list of varied assignments."

Randy has this advice for those hoping for an opportunity to enter a downshifted employment situation with their current employer:

"I was fortunate in that I had a good reputation as a person who gets things done. If people want to have the opportunity to stay with their company and perhaps be offered an option that isn't offered to everyone, they have to earn it. The way to do that is by developing skills that are important to the company and that are not easily replaceable. You have to continue to learn key skills. Assist new employees and fellow employees whenever you can. I trained many new employees in my time. What's more, you have to be visible. Get involved with new projects and make suggestions for improvements. Otherwise, it really doesn't pay for a company to let you work part-time while giving you full benefits."

Randy was ultimately let go in a general downsizing. (Another full disclosure: Teradyne gave Randy six months severance pay.) He is now involved in volunteer work in his community.

Sometimes the Decision Is Largely Practical

As interesting as work itself may be, the driving force behind working can be largely practical. Rick Harris, 65, an electrical engineer at Varian Medical Systems, can testify to that.

Rick started at Varian in 1996 as an operations manager. He worked on electronic imaging equipment that have applications in medicine, nondestructive testing (NDT), and security (x-raying packages for bombs, etc.). He enjoyed his work but was planning to retire in early 2004. Unfortunately, just at that point, Rick was diagnosed with colon cancer. In order to retain his company medical benefits, he needed to stay on the payroll. "I am eligible for Medicare, but the company's policy gives far more coverage," Rick explained. "Under Varian's retirement transition program, if I work 20 hours a week, I remain covered. I actually work up to 32 hours but due to my chemotherapy, sometimes I need to cut back."

One of the nice things about his new work status is that Rick is no longer a manager. "This is a creative business, and I enjoy being an individual contributing engineer," Rick noted. Even if Rick became independently wealthy tomorrow, he wouldn't leave Varian right away because "I couldn't just leave in the middle of a project. That wouldn't be right."

At Varian, the maximum time a person can remain in the retirement transition program is three years. "At that point I am going to build houses," Rick said. "I own some unimproved properties, and I look forward to speculating a bit in construction."

If you are considering bridge retirement, you need to realize two critical factors: (1) coming back on a part-time or short-term basis is a possibility, but *not a right or a guarantee*; (2) the company may be concerned about your ability to adjust to a less demanding job than you had before. For example, if you were used to making executive decisions and the job at hand is largely repetitive, there is some chance that you would be bored. That would be a loss for everyone involved. For that reason, a well-run program will interview people carefully to make sure that the retiree understands the daily reality of the work assignment.

For your current company to consider you as a good possibility for bridge employment, you will, of course, have to have a good work record. Furthermore, you will need to demonstrate that you understand the reasonable demands of a bridge assignment and how it may differ from your previous work experience.

Early Retirement: Taking the Package and Moving On

It is of course possible that some people will simply decide to retire completely given the right incentives of cash and enhanced pension benefits. These inducements can be very enticing. By one estimate, about 75 percent of those who do accept an early retirement offer indicate that they would not have retired when they did without this special inducement.

Let's set the scene. Your employer of 15 years is planning to downsize. At age 55, you are not planning to retire. Your employer offers an attractive early-retirement package, including severance pay. What do you do?

Donna Hutcheson, formerly of State Street Corporation in Boston, tells her story: "Employees had two months lead time in which to make a decision. For me there were several considerations. Since I have been married for 30 years, my husband's concerns were certainly a part of the picture. I had been making a nice salary, and he was concerned about losing the second paycheck. Talking it through, we concluded that we could get by on one paycheck if necessary by reining in our expenditures a bit. Our youngest child was finishing college, so that expense was going to be lifted from our shoulders anyway. Also, it is important to me personally to earn some of my own money, so I was concerned about how I would feel about not working. On the other hand, hanging over my head was the reality that I could be laid off anyway. Then I would lose both the early retirement package and my job."

After carefully weighing some additional factors, Donna decided to accept the package. "The terms of the package were generous, although I could not access my retirement fund until age 59½ without serious tax problems. On the other hand, there was a severance provision, which meant that my salary would continue for almost a year. Also, the timing was such that I could have an entire summer off for the first time in years. There was one more factor. I loved the company, but I did not enjoy a new assignment I had started 18 months before the retirement issue arose. Those relatively smaller factors played a role in my accepting the retirement package. Even so, it was not easy. I feel way too young to be retired. My father is 80 years old and is still working full-time."

What is next for Donna? "I want to work again because it gives me a purpose and a pattern. Not having a job to go to makes every evening seem like a Friday night, and that still feels a bit weird. On the other hand, our financial situation is such that I do not really need to figure out what to do next for about a year. Maybe I will find a contract opportunity in my field, which is human resources. Maybe I will try something else. In the meantime, I am glad that I have more time to volunteer at the local children's hospital."

There are good business reasons for a company to offer early retirement packages if they plan to downsize. First, those who accept the package are more likely to leave without bitter feelings. This is important for employers who want to avoid sabotage and/or the loss of proprietary information. Second, the company wants to reassure the remaining employees that they need not fear being thrown out of work summarily, without any kind of lifeline. Third, early retirement packages can be a hedge against age discrimination lawsuits.

Accepting an Offer of "Early Retirement"

Donna's experience with early retirement has been a positive one. What should you consider if your employer presents you with this option?

- **How secure is your job?** Will your job still be there if you *don't* accept the package? If your company is intent on downsizing, the next offer may not be as generous. In fact, you may be cut involuntarily in any event. If the offer is made to the entire company, your job may not be on the chopping block. If the offer is only to your specific division or functional area, your odds of being axed anyway are greater. Accepting the offer may therefore be viewed as a hedge against involuntary unemployment.

- **Is this an opportunity or a threat?** If you have been looking to leave your current employer to do something else (different job, more leisure), an early retirement offer can present a great opportunity. On the other hand, if you were planning to stay where you are based on financial necessity and/or job satisfaction, this could be a threat.

- **What is the honest viewpoint of your spouse or life partner?** You are not the only one impacted by your decision. Make sure that you have discussed the options openly and thoroughly with your spouse. His or her opinion may give you more latitude ("You don't have to accept this, honey. If worse comes to worse and you get laid off later, we still have my salary to live on.") or less latitude ("You need to accept this package, honey. Something now is better than the possibility of nothing later."). Either way, unless you are unattached, your decision impacts more than just yourself.

- **What is your time frame for making a decision?** Have you been given enough time to consult family members, a financial planner, and/or other interested individuals? If not, you may want to request more time to decide (albeit the request may not be granted).

Whatever your decision, you should seriously consider what you are going to do *next*. If you accept the package, do you have a plan for alternate professional pursuits or additional leisure that will be both satisfying and feasible? (According to one study, nearly a third of those who accepted an offer subsequently went to work for another employer.) If you do not accept the package, do you have a plan to seek alternate employment in case your job is cut?

In this chapter, we learned about bridge employment and early retirement. In chapter 3, we will take a look at contract employment as a working option.

Contract Employment: Opportunity, Variety, Insecurity

F OR SOME people, contract employment is attractive because of its practical advantages. One is the opportunity for professional growth. "Working for different employers exposes the contract employee to different ways of doing things and/or doing something they are familiar with in a different context," notes Jerry Erickson of ContractJobHunter.com. A second advantage is that your hourly wage is likely to be at a premium, perhaps 25 percent, over that of a direct employee doing similar work. The reason is that the contracting company is not responsible for medical insurance and pension expenses. In addition, there is no long-term commitment to you, and you can be dismissed without any legal hassle to the company.

A less tangible advantage for some people is the chance to travel and have new experiences. Some contract employees move about the country in an RV almost in the manner of an extended vacation. For married couples that have raised their children, this mode of earning a living may be especially attractive.

Many contract employees are in very technical professions, like engineering, but that is not always the case.

Susan Ascher (www.aschergroup.com), for example, specializes in contract employment for human resource (HR) professionals. "Since the HR function is not an income producer, it is becoming a highly outsourced profession," Susan notes. From the perspective of corporate clients, the most common time to look for contract HR help is when the company is about to ramp up hiring in a certain area. For example, let's say that the company anticipates hiring 100 new people in a data processing center. The company will want a recruiter to hire the new employees but does not want to be committed to his or her salary for an extended period. An experienced recruiter who can step in, get the hiring completed in six months, and then leave, seems to be the perfect solution from a budgeting point of view. Other HR functions that are finite projects are also good for contracting. For example, a company may contract an HR expert for six months to revise its compensation system from a salary-only to salary-plus-incentive system. Similarly, the contract employee might fill in for a benefits manager who is temporarily out on maternity leave.

Susan notes some additional benefits for the contract employee. "Perhaps she or he wants to do the job without having to worry so much about the career impact of corporate politics. For others, the contract situation may be a segue to a regular job. The transition from 'temp to perm' is not guaranteed, but it is not unusual either."

Here are some things you need to know if you are considering a contract situation:

- **Who is the employer?** Contract employees work through a contract staffing agency. The agency is the official employer. They will issue your paycheck and withhold income taxes and social security taxes. The contracting employer (the place where you actually work) is officially a client of the agency. Make sure that you know how long the agency has been in business because your paycheck will come from the agency. Similarly, ask the agency who their corporate clients are and if you can have the contact information for a few people who have used that agency to find employment. If the agency asks you to pay a fee, walk out the door.

- **How difficult is it to obtain contract employment?** The first contract assignment is often the hardest to get because it takes time to establish the appropriate contacts. It makes sense to contact a large number of contract-staffing agencies through websites and mailings because getting started is a bit of a numbers game.

- **On what basis is payment made?** Expect to be paid on an hourly basis. Your hourly wage, overtime compensation, and *per diem* arrangement (if any) is fixed by contract. On the other hand, the length of your assignment is approximate. You may be dismissed at any time. (Of course, you can also quit at any time.) In terms of income tax, at such time that you reasonably expect your assignment to last one year or longer, the IRS considers your assignment location to become your tax home.

- **What if I would really rather have a regular job but haven't found one yet?** Have a realistic attitude. First, a good job is better than a period of unemployment. Through a contract job, you can keep your skills sharp and your résumé current. Second, a contract job may pay you less than your last regular job. View that as a glass that is more than half-full and don't count the drops of water that are missing.

- **What can you tell me about the interview process?** In a sense, the recommendation of the contract-staffing agency is your interview. More often than not, the recruiter from the contract agency will speak with you on the telephone. It is not uncommon for a recruiter to be located hundreds, perhaps even thousands, of miles from the contractor. Therefore, a face-to-face interview may be impractical. For its part, the client company may accept you based on your résumé, coupled perhaps with a telephone interview. Do not misstate your qualifications or what you can do. In addition to the ethical issue, if the client finds out you cannot do the job, you can be dismissed summarily. Do not be surprised if a background check, a drug test, and a physical examination are part of the hiring process.

- **Who will supervise my employment?** There are some differences between a contract employee and a consultant. The contract employee is much like a direct employee. She or he is under the daily supervision and control of the client company.

Starting and Ending Contract Employment

Working as a contract employee means being just as professional as an employee. Some of the same general tips apply.

- *Do not feed into age-related stereotypes.* Dress smart. That means professional, well-tailored attire, and good personal grooming. An energetic demeanor is also an asset.
- *Anticipate periods of unemployment.* Therefore, it makes good sense to save some of what you earn for a rainy day.
- *Leave on good terms when you leave any client.* Common sense does not go out the window because your relationship has been relatively brief. Leaving on bad terms may hurt your chances with that company or another contract assignment in the future.

Let's take a look at the experiences of some folks who became contractors at age 55 or later:

When you speak with Jim Anthony, 60, he does not romanticize being a contract employee. "The fact is, I became a contract employee four or five years ago because it is just too difficult to be a regular employee in my field of technical writing. The employer has needs for your services, but they are not long-term. What's more, when the budget gets tight, technical writing is among the first things to go."

Jim worked for many years in the high tech industries based in New England, rising to the level of senior engineer. He was invited by a colleague to try technical sales, and it is here that Jim identified his passion. "I have a passion for teaching people, and technical sales was really about evangelizing the latest new technology and teaching people how easy it would be to design a product into the next generation computer. I loved what I was doing and did it for 15 years. Unfortunately, the computer manufacturing industry took a downturn in New England. I would have had to move to the West Coast to continue what I was doing."

When the local industry downsized, Jim tried other forms of selling. He tried real estate for a short period. That field relied more on building relationships than on teaching people, so it wasn't quite what Jim wanted. This is how Jim explained his next decision: "To make a living, I had to reinvent myself with something I would have a passion for, utilize my background experience, and make money, i.e., computers, software, and teaching."

"I then started my own business of selling my technical services to small retail businesses ($1–2 million or more in revenue size), installing and setting up a retail point-of-sale and inventory management system. I needed to find people who wanted to automate but didn't have the computer savvy. My objective was to be retained on an hourly basis, to act on a client's behalf with selecting appropriate equipment and software, installation and setup, and then teach people how to use it."

"I spent about two to three months getting started and learning everything about the hottest, inexpensive point-of-sale systems on the market (about 10). This was a great new career that only lasted one year with two good clients in the furniture business.

"I learned that I couldn't spend both 100 percent of my time with clients, always worrying about getting paid on time, and another 100 percent looking for new clients. I'd finish one client without any new clients ready to go and instead spent too much uncompensated time just looking for the next client."

When he realized that his own business was not going to be a paying proposition, Jim decided to "reinvent himself again" as a technical writer. "I collected everything I ever wrote and put together a sample portfolio along with a new résumé highlighting my few technical writing efforts over the past 20 years while being employed in a different type of career. This wasn't easy since I was competing with people having a lifetime career asking for less money." Jim did obtain short-term assignments, but again, that wasn't enough. "It appeared that my only option for making a reasonable income and to jump ahead of a crowded market was to quickly build a background through multiple employers, broad writing experiences, and obtaining multiple references. Contracting opportunities seemed like the only possibility. Promoting my writing skills along with my technical background enabled me to prevail."

Jim uses a number of methods to connect with clients. One is his own website (www.JimAnthony.com). "When a manager needs someone with my skills, they can find me by using a search engine like google.com. Then they can see examples of my work online before they even contact me." Jim has also posted his résumé on job sites like monster.com, and sometimes managers will find him by searching there. In addition, Jim has done some of his own outreach. "I created my own mailer and sent it to 1,200 people in 50 companies within commuting radius of my home. The mailer resulted in a few tepid inquiries but one solid hit. That's all I needed to secure the next six month assignment." Jim tries not to use agencies because "they would take too much of what I earn, sometimes 30 percent or more." Jim's depth of experience can mean that some contract assignments are extended when employers realize that he can do more for them than they originally considered. "Sometimes I finish a project to a client's satisfaction but then improve upon it on my own time. They get, let's say, 55 hours of work a week but billed only for 45. On the other hand, I am spending time on what amounts to my hobby and making a living at the same time. In addition, the improved product is part of my sales platform to secure my next assignment."

Although Jim loves what he does, he doesn't like the insecurity he has experienced. "There have been periods when I was out of work for three, four, or five months. That's not a great feeling, but I won't cave in on my rates. I make $50–$62 per billable hour and hope to climb to $75 in about a year if the economy continues to get better. If an employer is satisfied with a job I wouldn't put my name on, he could get away with paying only $30."

Jim has a number of thoughts about contracting that flow from his experience:

- **Passion:** "It is important to let your passion drive you. Otherwise you will just be a hired hand, making a dollar when you can."
- **Positioning:** "The only contractors that really make money are those who are actually 'consultants' and not a part-time employee."
- **Payment:** "When comparing your hourly rate to that of an equivalent direct employee, remember to factor in the health

> Like Jim Anthony, many contractors use P.A.C.E. (www.pace-pros.com), an organization that was founded in 1992. P.A.C.E. serves contract professionals as their employer of record and provides other services.

    insurance, pension benefits, and vacations that they get and you don't."

- **P.A.C.E:** "They are my back office and employer of record. I make far more money going through P.A.C.E. than contracting directly to a client."

From Corporate Professional to Happy Contract Employee

Let's say that you have been a human resource professional for over 25 years. You are now in your mid-50s. You love what you do and have gained an enormous amount of technical expertise. Then your employer, a large global chemical company, decides to restructure and to relocate its headquarters. What do you do?

Irene Monley of Wilmington, Delaware, was in that very position. "I had a passion for my work," Irene told me. "Employee benefits are important for the employee's financial security. A well-designed and well-communicated program also boosts morale and productivity. But when my company decided to move, I was not prepared to move with them."

Fortunately, Irene was well prepared professionally for her next step. "I had a very enlightened boss, and not everyone is that lucky. I asked for and ultimately was granted the opportunity to rotate among several departments within human resources. One of those areas was internal communications. By the time I finished all the rotations, I was appointed to a new position, director of employee benefits communications. That position did a lot for me. First, it gave me the skills I use now. Second, I worked with many consultants, giving me a good sense of how to approach my current work style. Third, my new role allowed me to stay with the company for a longer period because I played a vital role in the restructuring that was going on."

There was something else. Even when her formal employment ended, Irene's erstwhile employer asked her to stay on for another six months. "People grieve when they lose their job. The extra time made that process easier for me. Also, it introduced me to the idea of becoming a contract employee."

What does Irene do now and how does she get her clients? "I view myself as a communications consultant," Irene explained. "I help companies identify their strategic goals and use communications to achieve them. We examine their audience. That means thinking about the existing perceptions employees have, how they prefer to receive information, and what they already know. Then we develop the messages, identify the best modes of communication, and set up a timeline for what needs to be done. I become the project manager, writing the pieces and coordinating resources. I strive to deliver everything on time and within the established budget. When we have finished, we measure the results."

Irene's clients come from several sources. One is the extensive diaspora of former employees of Irene's old company. "They have gone elsewhere, but they remember the work I did when we were all at the chemical company." In addition, Irene has some name recognition in her field from years of work and from her involvement with a key professional association. "One reason to be involved is that I love the field and enjoy the people. The other reason is that visibility and name recognition help generate leads," Irene observed.

How much does Irene enjoy her current work style? "If someone offered me a regular job with a company, I would say, 'Let's try this on a contract basis first.'"

Thinking ahead, Irene is developing some special packages for smaller companies. "They don't have the same size budget as the larger companies, but they still need good communications with their employees. I am developing material that can be used almost as a template that a small company can modify easily to meet their specific need."

In chapter 3 we learned about contract employment. In chapter 4 we will take a look at franchising.

4

Franchising: Owning a Business with Someone Else's Shingle

O NE WAY to own and operate a business is to become a franchisee. In nonlegal terms, a franchise is an agreement between the owner of a process and someone who pays for the right to use that process. There are about 2,500 companies selling franchises in the United States today in a variety of industries including restaurants, convenience stores, automobile aftermarket (e.g., mufflers), and hotels.

Franchising is a popular option for some people because the franchisee is gaining access to a proven process. You do not have to be a path breaker. Instead, you need to be good at execution. In addition, the franchisee benefits from the advertising and marketing of the franchisor and will have some level of operational guidance available from a presumed expert in the field.

People of all age groups get involved in franchising. For the over 55-year-old set, some circumstances tend to be especially prevalent:

- **The laid-off executive:** Not surprisingly, as the economy turns down, the number of franchisees goes up. Some people who lose their job are determined never to work for someone else again and see a franchise as a means to independence.
- **The empty nester:** The kids are out of the house, so devoting time to a business now becomes more possible.

From the franchisor's point of view, selling franchises is a way to generate capital and to achieve growth through highly motivated people who have their own skin in the game. A reputable franchisor will sell a franchise only to someone who seems likely to succeed. That is why you may be asked many personal questions and may even be asked to take a personality or character test.

If you are thinking about becoming a franchisee, there are some important realities to consider;

- **It's not free:** You are buying the right to the franchisor's process for a specified number of years. You must pay a franchise fee. Then there is a royalty payment, which is a percentage of your revenue in addition to a contribution to the overall company's advertising fund.
- **It's not easy:** Expect to put in 12- to14-hour days if you want to succeed. Also, expect to be on the premises a good deal of the time. Expect long workdays, with much of your time spent on the premises.
- **It's not always glamorous:** You may be the one flipping the burgers, cleaning the cars, etc., especially when your part-time help forgets to show up.
- **It's not always profitable:** You may take home no more than you could have made as an employee. If substantial income is to flow, you may need to own more than one unit. Of course,

that requires additional investment and more of your time. If the franchise is just a way of having a job, you could be better off investing the money and working for someone else.

- **It's not without financial pitfalls:** A younger person may have time to make up any losses. At your age, you are betting your pension. It makes sense to be more conservative and risk adverse.

- **It's not about sole decision-making:** Make sure that your spouse is in agreement with the project. It is going to be time-consuming, energy absorbing, and financially risky. You may need to have your spouse working in the business, at least early on. Also, your franchise may not be a legacy. By the time you are 55 or 65, your children may already have begun to establish their own careers.

Still interested?

- Start researching the possibilities by reading trade journals like the *Franchise Times* (www.franchisetimes.com).
- Assess the degree to which you can afford to take a risk. Also assess how long and hard you are willing to work.
- Retain a good franchise lawyer. One good source is the American Bar Association (www.abanet.org).
- Try to work part-time in the business you are considering before taking the leap.
- Make sure that you have the support of your spouse, family, and friends. It is even harder to put in the long hours and deal with the difficulties without the support of those close to you.

After you approach a franchisor, you should be sent a Uniform Franchise Offering Circular (UFOC). This document should include a list of particulars about the business offering. In addition, there must be a list of other franchisees. Contact some of them. You should ask them how their business is doing, challenges they are facing, and if the franchisor is fair and helpful or a source of problems. The UFOC also will list litigation. This is a good source of information to see what other kinds of problems the franchisor has faced with its franchisees.

The Process: GNC as a Case in Point

For a reputable company, choosing the right franchisees is an important part of doing business. At GNC, the nation's largest specialty retailer of nutritional supplements, the process is both extensive and intensive. From the pool of 1,000 inquiries the company receives each month, about 60 will be offered the opportunity to franchise a GNC. According to J.J. Sorrenti, senior vice president and general manager, there are three formal steps in the process at GNC:

- **Get Acquainted form:** Through this document, the company seeks four things. *First,* expansion potential. The company places a high value on rewarding multiple locations to operators who have proven their ability to provide an exceptional customer experience. *Second,* is the applicant nutrition and/or fitness oriented? It is important to have franchisees that are sincerely interested in helping their customers live well. *Third,* will the prospective franchisee be committed full-time to operating the store? *Fourth,* is the applicant financially qualified? (The cost of the franchise in 2004 was $150,000, which can be partially financed by the company. Annual royalties come to 6 percent of gross revenues.)

- **Formal application:** The application provides GNC a detailed snapshot of how the candidate measures up against GNC's qualification standards.
- **Face-to-face meeting:** This is an all-day meeting at GNC headquarters in Pittsburgh. The meeting is a chance to review the details of the franchise relationship and for applicants to gain a thorough understanding of the brand, the operating system, and the ongoing support GNC provides—while getting to know some of the people at GNC who will be available to support their efforts. GNC gets a sense of the applicant's trustworthiness (after all, he or she will be representing the GNC brand), commitment to excellence, and caring about the customer as an individual. Further, they would like to know that the potential franchisee has a personality that will let him or her succeed within the established system. Unlike the person who owns their own business, franchisees cannot be renegades.

GNC has found that its franchisees are more successful than its corporate stores, probably because the franchisee has made the ultimate commitment of his or her own money. Older franchisees may also be more serious about the enterprise and more committed to the care of their customers.

Extra Considerations for the Older Franchisee

Older franchisees must be especially sure that they have an exit strategy. What are you going to do with your business when you are ready to leave it? As the company's franchise system has matured, GNC has seen many franchise operators plan a legacy, namely leaving their business to their children. But you must be aware of your individual case. Would your children actually be interested in running the business?

Let's take a look at the actual experiences of two franchisees.

Franchising for the Family

In 1989, at age 55, Don Shanks retired for a while. He had been the vice president for customer relations at Piedmont Airlines. The airline merged, Don accepted an early retirement package, and off he went. Along with his wife, Don traveled by motorcycle touring the lower 48 states and most of Canada.

Don got into franchising for family reasons. His son was in manufacturing, and manufacturing was in decline. In order to help his son establish a more secure income, Don chose to franchise a GNC store in Kernersville, North Carolina, just as his brother had done successfully in Tennessee some years prior. "I told my son to keep his day job and work in the store when he could. His mother and I would get the business up and running for him to take over." That first store worked out so well that Don and his family have opened three more.

Initially Don was putting in a 60-hour workweek. "If you are not ready to do that, don't expect to succeed," he noted. Part of the reason was that he enjoyed working with customers so much that "sometimes it was just tough to leave." The other reason for so many hours is the amount of work that needs to be done. "We unloaded trucks, unpacked boxes, stocked the shelves. The list of tasks is pretty long."

The transition from corporate life wasn't easy. "At Piedmont, if I had a staffing issue, I called HR. For a legal question, I called the law department. The accounting department took care of all the accounting. When you are running a store, that falls on you," Don observed. Being a franchisee can also have some frustrations. When you have a boss, you do what she or he directs. When you have your own business, you do what you think is best. A franchisee is in between. "You may get a directive about stocking shelves in a certain manner. You say to yourself, 'My goodness, this is my store, and in this town it would make more sense to do it a different way.'

You can make your concerns known, but GNC wants all of its stores to be consistent. In the end you accept company policy on things of that nature."

Franchising a Business to Business Service

Sometimes a franchise can provide a service to businesses, rather than consumers. It can also provide experiences that may have been missing in the salaried employment world.

Dick Stumbo of Reno, Nevada, was the chief financial officer for several exchange-listed companies over a 20-year period including one on the Fortune 500 list. When he retired (for the second time) at age 60, Dick was secure financially but looking for something productive and interesting to do with his time.

"It had to be something I could do well and enjoy," Dick recalled. "I heard about some accounting/bookkeeping franchisees and decided to check them out." Dick examined the four main franchisors in the field. "One wouldn't give me any information, so that ruled them out. A second targeted businesses whose owners were not as sophisticated as I would want. The third was pretty good but didn't quite have what I was looking for. The fourth, then called Comprehensive Business Services, had the target clients and the operating methods that I wanted," Dick explained.

Dick thought the matter through. The franchisor had marketing skills that weren't Dick's strong point and marketing tools to attract clients that Dick could develop on his own. There was also the attraction of owning his own business. Dick came on board.

There were a few unpleasant surprises that didn't overwhelm Dick but may have been more significant to others with less drive and experience. The franchisor's proprietary computer software was not current, and the number of qualified leads to new clients the franchisor provided were fewer than Dick had expected. Even so, Dick loved the experience. "My greatest joy was spending so much time with clients. Efficient business practice might say too much time, but it gave me a dimension of business and personal interaction that was something I didn't have as a big company CFO," Dick remarked.

Dick grew the business but sold it three years later at a point where it was just becoming profitable. "I am a bit of a workaholic, and I was spending 80–100 hours a week on my business. Sometimes you have to put a value on having some time to yourself. The other thing is that I delegated too much for a small business (quite different than a large corporation). Especially after my daughter decided to leave the business, I was doing a lot more of the mundane activities than I really wanted to do. Also the sheer thrill of owning my own business was beginning to diminish," Dick said looking back.

If Dick were giving advice to a friend who was 55 years old or older who asked about buying a franchise, this is what he would say:

- If, at or near my age, you are doing this for income, you would probably be better off working for a salary and holding on to the franchise fee as an interest or dividend generator.
- A franchise requires an enormous amount of work. Do you still have the amount of energy you used to?
- If you are thinking about a franchise just to see if you can run a business, make sure you know what it takes to run a business.
- Make sure there is a way out. Sometimes you can sell your franchise only under restricted conditions, and you had better consider that up front.

Dick enjoyed his franchise experience and sometimes wonders if he would have been happier starting it earlier. In any event, he has

Here are some good sources of information on franchising.

- The American Franchisee Association (www.franchisee .org): This Chicago-based association is the oldest and largest trade association representing small business franchisees in the United States.
- The Franchise Equity Group (www.fegroup.org): Articles outlining a franchisee's legal rights, the benefits and drawbacks of joint ventures, tax issues, and how to increase the equity in a franchise investment can be found at this website.
- Federal Trade Commission Franchise Information (www .ftc.gov/bcp/franchise/netfran.htm): This website features information about things to look for when buying a franchise.
- Forum on Franchising (www.abanet.org/forums/franchising): American Bar Association Franchising Forum addresses issues relating to franchising laws.
- The Franchise Network (www.frannet.com): This website, produced by the Network of Franchise Consultants, features how-to information about selecting the franchise that's right for you.

You can find information about specific franchising opportunities at these websites:

- Center court (www.centercourt.com): You can find some useful information in addition to publicity about franchise opportunities through this organization.

(continued)

- Entrepreneur Magazine Business Opportunity 500 (www .entrepreneur.com): Visitors to this website can search for business opportunities in a variety of categories.
- The Franchise Annual On-line (www.infonews.com): This website features a comprehensive franchise directory.
- Franchise Solutions (www.franchisesolutions.com): Franchise and other business opportunities, along with basic information about buying and selling a business are featured on this website.
- Franchise Update (www.franchise-update.com): This website features information about the industry and franchise business opportunities.
- The Franchise Handbook (www.franchise1.com): This website features fact sheets about popular franchises, business opportunities, and the latest news bites from the franchise industry.
- FranInfo (www.Franinfo.com/default.html): Visitors to this website will find information about buying and selling franchises, creating franchises, and franchising opportunities.

continued with what he enjoyed most, working with clients, which he now does on a voluntary basis.

Franchise Considerations

There are thousands of franchising opportunities in the United States. However, not all of these opportunities make good business sense. Kay Marie Ainsley, a franchising consultant (Kainsley@ msaworldwide.com), has this advice about determining the "franchisability" of a business:

- The business has an operating history and is not just a concept. (Remember, the franchisee is buying the right to use an operating system—most prospective franchisees are best advised to look for a system that has been tested and proven.)
- The business can be duplicated—operating systems are in place, and others can easily be taught to operate the business. Although you will need to know how to do everything, you don't want to be the only person capable of doing anything.
- The business is using franchising as a means to expand—franchising is not needed for the company's survival.
- The economics of the business will work for both the franchisor and the franchisee.
- A sufficient market demand exists for the product or service being offered (the company who makes leis probably shouldn't try to franchise outside of Hawaii).
- The company has the rights or can obtain the rights to the name under which the business will operate.
- The culture of the company is conducive to establishing a strong relationship with its franchisees. Ask the franchisor for a list of franchisees you can interview.
- The company can provide sustainable value to its franchisees on an ongoing basis.
- A sufficient pool of potential qualified franchisees is likely to be had, and the franchise opportunity created by the company will be marketable and competitive with other franchise opportunities.
- The franchisor and their staff are likeable people. It's best if you have confidence that they will provide the leadership needed to grow the business and to guide the system through tough times, if necessary.

THINKING ABOUT STARTING YOUR OWN BUSINESS?

Some people who want to own a business want it to be their *very own*, not a franchise. Here are some things to consider:

People may become entrepreneurs at any age. Younger people may want to be their own boss or try out a new idea when they have a minimum of other responsibilities. Older people also may want to be free of bosses or pursue an idea, especially if their major responsibilities to others have passed.

You will probably not be another Ray Kroc (McDonald's) or Colonel Sanders (KFC), who were age 53 and 65, respectively, when they undertook their famous entrepreneurial ventures. In fact, you may not make all that much money. On the other hand, you may get the satisfaction of a lifetime from your own business. It is your own vision, and you have given birth to it.

If you are contemplating starting your own business, here are some tips for you:

- **Start with something you know:** For example, a former elementary school teacher may consider a day care or after-school center.
- **Develop a serious business plan:** This is not just a "must-do" in order to raise money. You need to parse out the details of where you think you are going, who your customers or clients will be, who the competition is, and how you will deal with the variety of economic conditions you may confront.
- **Beware of glamorous or romantic visions:** A typical misstep is to think that owning a restaurant would be glamorous. This exacting business requires a huge amount

of personal effort in addition to capital investment. Most restaurants fail.

- **Be cautious:** You have less time to recoup if your investment fails.
- **Stay current with the field:** Be sure to read both the general entrepreneurial press, like *Entrepreneur Magazine* (www.entrepreneur.com), and the trade journals specific to your field.

What about starting your own business when you are older? I asked Erv Simon, who has been a volunteer counselor for SCORE for 10 years.

Older people are often less driven by the need to make money and more driven by the desire to do something that they have put off doing. For example, a man who always wanted to own a garden shop opened one with his wife. They built up the business until they owned three garden centers. Ultimately, they sold the centers to their children.

On the other hand, some people start out with the question, "What can I do?" Perhaps they have been laid off and see scant prospects of paid employment in their previous line of work.

Erv asks people, "What is your passion?" If it is not your passion, it won't be a successful business. If you are watching the clock, you are in the wrong business.

People need to be realistic about required time commitments. If you are opening a business just for the joy of it, a 40-hour workweek may suffice. If you are looking to replace a previous source of income, 60–80 hours a week is probably necessary. In a sense, there is never enough time, and therefore you need to

(continued)

manage the time you have as well as possible. What you *can* do may be less than what you *should* do. Learning what you shouldn't do is also important.

Older people tend to be better able to make a rational business plan than younger folks, perhaps because they have more life experience. On the other hand, those who have never run a business often don't realize that there are two or even three dimensions: (1) the front side that faces the customer, (2) the back office, and often, (3) the production area.

In terms of money, older folks may well have enough money put away, whereas younger people usually don't have ready capital. Still the older folks need to ask themselves if they are willing to put their capital at risk. In that regard, one consideration is that older people have less time to recoup if their business fails.

In Erv's view, if you are debating whether to start your own business or become a franchisee, consider this maxim: the business owner loves to run his own show, the freedom to experiment. The franchisee tends to love (or at least be able to live with) a routine that has been established by the franchisor.

In this chapter we took a look at franchising as an option for those over the age of 55. In chapter 5, we will take a look at volunteering as a meaningful option.

Volunteering: The Payback Is Not in the Paycheck

ACCORDING TO a recent study, "Fifty-six percent of Americans between the ages of 50 and 75 are planning to make volunteering and community service part of their post-career life." (Peter D. Hart Research Associates on behalf of Civic Ventures). If volunteers were paid, volunteering would be a $260 billion per year industry.

Many people give themselves to a cause out of a sense of social purpose. It should be noted, however, that volunteering may be good for the volunteer *socially, emotionally, and physically.* Numerous studies have indicated that volunteering may bring the following benefits to the older volunteer:

- A chance to use your talents
- Feeling good about doing good
- Feeling valued while giving something back
- A greater likelihood of feeling optimistic about the future

- A sense that your older years are a new chapter in your life
- Staying connected or getting reconnected to others
- Providing intellectual stimulation
- A chance to do something you couldn't do before
- Encouraging physical activity
- A way to do something significant with your time
- Promoting better health (attributable at least in part to the other benefits mentioned here)
- A sense that you can control your situation because you can walk away from it if necessary

Unfortunately, some volunteers find that they are assigned to menial tasks that are not intrinsically fulfilling. There are times when volunteers may be seen as a class distinct from (and beneath) paid employees. What can you do to make sure that your volunteer experience is a positive one?

First, treat the situation like a job search. Research and apply for several volunteer opportunities and choose the one that best utilizes your interests and skills. These might be skills you used in your paid jobs or skills you never had a chance to use before. *Second,* ask what the organization's volunteer philosophy is. You want to know that they will value you for your skills and not simply use you for cheap labor. *Third,* be clear what your duties would be. A well-run organization should have a specific job description for you. Similarly, you should ask when your performance will be reviewed and what the criteria will be. An organization that reviews your performance is more likely to value your service. *Fourth,* make sure that your goals and motivations are consistent with the opportunity. For example, if you want to be working directly with people, and the volunteer assignment is working in an isolated work space, that doesn't seem to be a good match. Further, if you need some flexibility in your work schedule, but the organization needs people who will reliably and consistently meet a fixed schedule, it may not be a good match. *Fifth,* find out if volunteers receive some kind of recognition. This might mean a recognition dinner, stories about volunteers in the organization's newsletter, or even a modest stipend. If a stipend is involved (let's say $200 per month) find out if you need to work a minimum number of hours per week to be eligible. For many people, the stipend may be more than just the cherry on top of a meaningful experience. It may be a needed supplement to a small income. *Sixth,* be realistic. If you are used to being a highly paid executive, you will have to adjust to a situation where you are not giving directives. If other volunteers have been with the organization longer, they may have priority for more interesting assignments. Although many people will appreciate your contributions, some people will not take any special notice.

Where can you look for a good volunteer opportunity? Here are some sources you can check out on the Internet. (If you don't have Internet access at home, you may be able to utilize a computer at your local library or senior center.)

■ **VolunteerMatch** (www.VolunteerMatch.org): "Volunteer-Match is a nonprofit organization with a mission to help everyone find a great place to volunteer and offers a variety of online services to support a community of nonprofit, volunteer and business leaders committed to civic engagement. Interested volunteers can enter their zip code on the VolunteerMatch home page to quickly find local volunteer opportunities posted by nonprofit organizations throughout the United States."

(continued)

- **Experience Corps** (www.experiencecorps.org): "Experience Corps® offers new adventures in service for Americans over 55. Now in 13 cities, Experience Corps works to solve serious social problems, beginning with literacy. Today more than 1,500 Corps members serve as tutors and mentors to children in urban public schools and after-school programs, where they help teach children to read and develop the confidence and skills to succeed in school and in life. Research shows that Experience Corps boosts student academic performance, helps schools and youth-serving organizations become more successful, strengthens ties between these institutions and surrounding neighborhoods, and enhances the well-being of the volunteers in the process. Experience Corps is a signature program of Civic Ventures."

- **Senior Corps** (www.seniorcorps.org): "Senior Corps is a network of programs that tap the experience, skills, and talents of older citizens to meet community challenges with Foster Grandparents, Senior Companions, and RSVP (Retired and Senior Volunteer Program)."

- **Corporation for National and Community Service** (www.nationalservice.org): "The Corporation for National and Community Service engages Americans of all ages and backgrounds in service to help strengthen communities."

- **USA Freedom Corps Volunteer Network** (www .usafreedomcorps.gov): "You can use the USA Freedom Corps Volunteer Network to find volunteer opportunities at home or abroad. Just enter geographic information, such as zip code or state, and your area of interest,

so you can access service opportunities near your home
or office, across the country, or overseas."

- In addition, your local community may have volunteer
centers and many churches, synagogues, and mosques
sponsor services provided by volunteers.

Note: There are a number of government funded Senior
Community Service Employment Programs (SCSEP). These
are work-training programs for low-income persons age 55
and older. They help those in need to retrain for a changing
workforce, to find self-confidence, and most importantly, to
find a job. You can learn more at www.aarp.org/scsep or www
.experienceworks.org/scsep.html.

Let's take a look at some older Americans and their volunteer
experiences. The first story is about a person who stayed close to
home.

What do you do after a lifetime of volunteering for your church
and school, after years of taking care of your family? If you are
Kathleen Saragosa of San Diego, California, you volunteer to help
people from a very different community than your own. For three
mornings a week, she works with 20 or so women who are under
lockdown in a place called Casa San Juan. Their crime is being in
the United States illegally, and they are being held pending final
processing. While some may be permitted to remain in the U.S.,
others will be deported to their homelands of Mexico, China, and
many countries in South America.

"I lived in a Mexican-American community in Carpinteria,
California, for 40 years, so I am familiar with many aspects of the
Hispanic community. My role is mostly being a teacher and a

facilitator," Kathleen explained. "Trying to do things with these women that will make them feel better—like sewing. It helps pass the time and makes them feel they are doing something productive. Some women have even said to me that they plan to buy their own sewing machine when they get back home and make crafts."

Kathleen studied art, Spanish, and early childhood development in college, and she enjoys employing those skills now. "I did accounting and bookkeeping for a living. Helping these women gives me a chance to apply skills I learned and loved but never had a chance to use professionally."

Volunteering on the Move

Sometimes volunteering can be a really moving experience—from Kauai, Hawaii, to Olympia, Washington; from Fort Myers, Florida, to Tucson, Arizona; from Lawrence, Massachusetts, to Alliance, Ohio. George and Diane Gravlee have built homes for Habitat for Humanity in 27 states through the RV Care-A-Vanner organization (www.habitat.org/gv/rv/html). George, now 64, is a former federal government hydrologist, who took early retirement 10 years ago. Diane, 61, is a former school librarian. They had always enjoyed travel and the outdoors. When they thought about what to do with their life after work, they asked a question that guides them throughout life in general, "What would God want us to do?" In 1994, they had sent Habitat for Humanity a small donation and received its newsletter. It had a notice asking for 125 volunteers to build houses in Hawaii to replace homes that had been destroyed by a hurricane. "That looked like a great place to see if building would be for us," Diane recalled.

Kauai, Hawaii, was not beautiful when George and Diane arrived. It was devastated. "These were people in real need. We could see the dividends from our efforts because a family, living on the beach for a year and working side by side with us, was now going to own a home," George noted. "The family's tears of joy gave us a great sense of accomplishment. That experience has led us to over 70 other builds. We do about seven two-week builds a year, and we hope to eventually do at least one in each of the 50 states."

George and Diane, who happen to live full-time in their RV now, belong to a growing fellowship of RV Care-A-Vanners. "We have so much in common that we just want to stay in touch," Diane observed. "Not all the volunteers are out there hammering with us; local affiliates need fund-raisers, site-finders, office workers, and lunch-makers as well." Some of the people George and Diane build with are two generations younger, such as when they supervise college students under the Alternative Spring Break program. "It keeps us young, and we have even been roller-skating with them when the workday was done," Diane laughed. "Young people can be fun to watch because they are so surprised to find out that they can actually build something with their hands," George added.

George has always been handy around the house, but for Diane, there has been an extra bonus. She can do a great many things she never tried before. "I can hang sheet rock, do framing, install vinyl siding . . . everything except the roofing because I don't like heights," she said with pride. "If you don't know how to do a task, somebody is there to teach you."

One of the fringe benefits of Habitat for Humanity for Diane and George is that it has helped them stay healthy. "We get some exercise," Diane commented. "At the same time, you have to know your limitations," George added. "Do what you can and pace yourself throughout the day. Some folks enjoy the robust activity of building walls and putting roofs on. Others prefer the careful detailed jobs of hanging doors, installing baseboard, and painting. There is something for everyone."

The Habitat for Humanity experience may not be for everyone. As Diane noted, "One person's fun is another person's work. But we've found building with Habitat for Humanity a wonderful experience and have been blessed by it."

Sharing Your Wealth of Experience

What do you do after working with 50 different companies in businesses ranging from insurance to wood stoves? If you are Walter Pastuszak, 64, of Chicopee, Massachusetts, you help other people benefit from your wealth of experience.

"When I was working, I loved solving problems and developing people. I did that as a manager, corporate vice president, and as a consultant," Walt explained. "I enjoyed making a difference then, and that is one of the things I like doing now."

Walt's transition from the marketplace to volunteering started with two factors: he could afford it, and after 9/11, his market for consulting was drying up. "I said, the heck with it, I'm retired!" One of Walt's friends asked him to do some consulting with SCORE (Service Corp. of Retired Executives, www.score.org). This meant a minimum commitment of two face-to-face counseling sessions per month. "I had free time, it was February, and I was looking for something to do when my friend asked," Walt put it succinctly. His clients are people who need advice on business issues, ranging from the most basic steps of a possible start-up to facing a difficult challenge in an existing business. Walt also gives advice through e-mail. "That can be especially interesting and challenging," Walt noted. "The clients could be from anywhere in the country. They may pose a problem that is new for me, so I do some background research. Even if I can't give a solution directly, I can direct the client to a good source that can."

Walt's counseling has produced many success stories. For example, his recommendations after reviewing their business plans helped several people secure loans through the Small Business Administration. Another client was able to avoid foreclosure when their business ran into trouble. "Many clients have and continue to send thank-you notes indicating that my advice provided them the direction they needed on imports, exports, setting up credit accounts, business planning, and a myriad of other subjects," Walt noted with pride.

Walt feels that volunteering for SCORE gives him the sense of satisfaction he wants without the constraints of a paying job. "If I want to go away for a while, I can just take myself off-line. That way, I won't be in the 48-hour response loop for online clients. I also have time for my hobbies like tennis, golf, and photography." Volunteering is also a great antiaging tonic. "When you keep learning, you keep growing. When you stop growing, you get old," Walt observed.

In this chapter we learned more about the benefits of volunteering. Chapter 6 will start taking an extensive look at the process of finding a new job.

Four Steps to Your Next Job

N THIS CHAPTER, we will take a look at what you need to do if you are going back into the labor market in whatever capacity (employee, consultant, etc.). There are **four key steps**: identifying what you want and your priorities; building your skills inventory; knowing where and how to look for a job; and getting started.

1. Identifying Wants and Priorities

It is much easier to obtain what you want if you know what it is and why you want it. This requires some introspection, which many people find difficult. To make things easier, answer the basic questions below.

1. If you had to put your reasons for working on a bumper sticker, what would you say:

a. I need the money
b. I enjoy working
c. I want to use my skills
d. I want something to do with my time
e. I want to stay connected with other people
f. Other (please indicate in ten words or less)

_____

g. Several of the above (please identify which ones):

_____

2. How many hours a week do you *want* to work? What is the *maximum* number of hours you would be willing to work?

_____

3. Do you want a work situation similar to the one you just left, something substantially different, or does it not matter?

_____

4. Are you willing to make less money than you made before?

_____

5. How much of a daily commute are you willing to make?

_____

6. Are you interested in a specific company? If so, which one?

_____

7. Are you interested in a specific industry? If so, which one?

_____

8. Are you interested in a specific type of job? What would be some possible job titles?

_____

9. Describe your idea of the perfect next job in a few sentences:

_____

_____

_____

_____

_____

10. What aspects of your *perfect* job are you willing to forgo to obtain an *acceptable* job?

_____

_____

_____

_____

_____

Based on your answers to the 10 questions above, you can now develop a list of priorities for your next job. Let's establish three categories: Must have, nice to have, and can't have. For example, this is what Gabrielle wrote:

Must have
Salary of at least $35,000
Pleasant coworkers
Minimal stress

Nice to have
Be in my previous industry
Use my previous training
Have an office rather than production environment
Have flexible leave time policy

Shouldn't have/can't have
A commute of more than 45 minutes
More than a 40-hour workweek
Customer service orientation

Gabrielle took this process a step further by prioritizing her items in each category. For example, in the "Must Have" category, she determined that her priorities were: minimal stress, salary of at least $35,000, and pleasant coworkers.

2. Building a Solid Skills Inventory

Building a skills inventory has several important advantages for you. First, it will help you write a good, interview-winning résumé. Second, when you do interview, you will have a solid basis for presenting the skills you have that match what the employer needs. Third, when you articulate your set of skills you will be able to identify more job opportunities for which you can apply.

I recommend that you approach this from two directions, your own experiences and where you want to go next:

- **Make a list of skills and attributes that you feel good about in yourself:** You may want to use your own recent job description or performance evaluation as resources. In addition, ask a friend or colleague for some positive feedback about you. (There is no reason to be shy about this. You may take for granted, and therefore overlook, many skills that others notice.) After you have written your list of skills and attributes, write at least one example to substantiate each one.

Example: *Analyzed flow of goods from warehouse to stores. Determined which parts of the supply chain were the most vulnerable to shrinkage. Based on analysis, suggested changes that resulted in 10 percent reduction in shrinkage.* (Your example will be especially useful if you include results.)

- **Carefully read a description for a job that you may want to pursue:** Write down each skill or attribute the description mentions. Then write a short sentence indicating an example of you demonstrating that skill or attribute.

Example: Let's say, you find a description for a job that interests you, and it indicates that "excellent writing skills" are required. If writing is not already in your skills inventory, add it. As a supporting example you might write:

Wrote report detailing the relative merits of proposed new product design based on econometric data and customer preference forecasts.

- **Note:** Some of the examples you develop in your skills inventory will fit well in the experience section of your résumé. An even larger part of your skills inventory will be useful at your job interviews.

3. Finding Those Who Can Help

Networking

Here are two job search truths that apply at any age: nobody should go into a job search alone, and networking still works. Unfortunately, some people who reach their 50s, 60s, and 70s are reluctant to ask for help. Remember that it feels good to be a giver, so allow someone a chance to achieve that good feeling by helping you. Besides, someday you may well return the favor. Let's think about people who can help you.

If you currently have a job and are looking for another, your spouse should know about your plans. After all, he or she is your partner in life and will be affected by your decision. Your closest, most confidential friends could be told but use your judgment. After all, people do talk. Unfortunately, some bosses will force you to leave prematurely and unwillingly if they get wind of your plans.

If you are not currently working, or your plans for seeking a new job do not need to be a secret, then your family, friends, and colleagues (past and present) should be informed. At the least, they can offer moral support, a valuable element in dealing with the difficult emotional and practical aspects of a job search.

People who may be willing to help you with advice, insights, and perhaps even leads to specific jobs are your job search network. I encourage you to think of your network in broad terms. It should include not only your friends, family, and neighbors, but also family of friends and friends of family, etc. Similarly, your personal network should include not only your nuclear family but also aunt, uncles, cousins, nieces, nephews, in-laws, and steprelations. I would also include other people with whom you have a close relationship, such as your pastor, physician, attorney, accountant, and financial advisor.

How Should You Approach People?

First, remember that you are approaching people *for advice*, not a job lead, let alone a job interview. When you ask for advice, people don't feel backed into an uncomfortable position. If they have something to suggest, they can. If not, they can tell you that. (Of course, it is your responsibility to evaluate the advice you get.)

Second, start with people you are close to, like family and friends. They may be more comfortable to approach, and they will be glad to hear from you. One thing you can ask is if they have friends, neighbors, or colleagues who might be willing to speak with you. In that way, you can expand the scope of your network.

Third, once you are comfortable approaching people for advice, contact people in the industry, profession, or company of interest to you, who you don't know personally. They could be friends of relatives, or they could be complete strangers, in which case I recommend writing before calling. It is fine to use either an e-mail or a letter for this purpose. John was thinking about getting a full-time job in mall management. A simple call to the local mall office yielded the name and e-mail address of the manager. Here is the text of the e-mail John sent:

Vernon Rapp:

I am in the process of exploring a career change. Mall management is a field that interests me, and I would appreciate your insights and suggestions about the pragmatic issues involved with this career. Could you spend 15–20 minutes with me to discuss this industry?

Let me give you some personal background. Most recently, I have been a manager in a freight shipping company. That company has downsized, and I am now looking for other avenues for my talents. Mall management has attracted me because my research to date indicates that it would draw on my professional skills while offering some new challenges.

I will call you in a few days with the hope that you can offer me the benefit of your advice. Let me assure you that I am seeking your ideas, not a job interview.

John Johnson

Notice that John is under no obligation to say anything about his age, nor should he express any concerns he might have in this letter. John simply and briefly asks for what he wants, namely advice, while giving a little background on himself.

As John promised in his e-mail, he called a few days later, asking to arrange for an informational interview.

WHAT DID JOHN ASK?

John brought some questions with him when he met with Vernon Rapp. (A face-to-face meeting is best for getting good information and for establishing contact. Telephone is the next best option.) Here is what John was prepared to ask:

- I really appreciate that you have taken the time to speak with me this morning. My first question is this: I would like to know how you got started in this career. I am especially interested in knowing what attracted you to this field.
- Please tell me some of the things you like best in your job and some of the things you would rather do without.
- I would like to know how you spend your time on the job. Can you describe a typical day or week?
- What are the skills a person needs to succeed in this profession?
- Can you tell me how you feel when work starts on Monday and ends on Friday? In fact, given the nature of the job, do you also work on weekends?
- How does your job add value to your company? Who are the people you work with in the course of a week?
- Is there a career ladder in mall management? If so, what would be a possible next career step for a successful person like yourself?
- If I came to you and said, "I am thinking about going into this field," what advice would you give me?
- Can you suggest some additional people I might speak with as I explore this career further?

Identifying Potential Employers

Although networking may be your best single approach, it should not be your only approach. Here are some resources you can use. (*Note:* If you are not familiar with how to access or use these resources, you may find that the librarian at your local library is more than willing to be of assistance. Many local libraries have Internet access that is available to the public.)

JOB SEARCH WEBSITES

Here are some of the websites that you could use, along with a brief statement of how they describe themselves:

- **www.thingamajob.com/:** "At Thingamajob, we're actually doing the hiring. Thingamajob is a free online employment resource provided by the Allegis Group, parent company to some of the world's largest staffing companies including Aerotek, TEKsystems, and Mentor 4, Inc. Thingamajob helps the Allegis Group family of staffing companies recruit the best talent, *people just like you*, for positions with Fortune 1000 companies."
- **www.monster.com/:** "Get Work. Network. Do it all with Monster. Find a great job. Meet the right people. Make big things happen for yourself and your career. We'll show you how."
- **www.ajb.dni.us/:** "The biggest and busiest job market in cyberspace. Job seekers can post their résumé where thousands of employers search every day, search for job

(continued)

openings automatically, and find their dream job fast. Employers can post job listings in the nation's largest online labor exchange, create customized job orders, and search résumés automatically to find the right people fast."

- **www.driagslist.com:** This easy to navigate website provides job listings and accesses many other categories of information and discussion.

- **hotjobs.yahoo.com/:** "As a leader in the online recruiting industry, Yahoo! HotJobs has revolutionized the way people manage their careers and the way companies hire talent. Yahoo! HotJobs' tools and advice put job seekers in control of their careers and make it easier and more cost-effective for employers and staffing firms to find qualified candidates. In addition to its popular consumer job board, Yahoo! HotJobs provides employers, recruiters, and staffing agencies with progressive recruiting solutions and hiring management software."

- www.careerbuilder.com/: "CareerBuilder.com is the nation's leading online job network with more than 15 million unique visitors and over 600,000 jobs. Owned by Gannett Co., Inc. (NYSE: GCI), Tribune Company (NYSE: TRB), and Knight Ridder, Inc. (NYSE: KRI), the company offers a vast online and print network to help job seekers connect with employers. CareerBuilder.com powers the online career centers for more than 400 partners that reach national, local, industry, diversity, and niche audiences. These include more than 130 newspapers and leading portals such as America Online and MSN. More than 30,000 of the nation's top employers take advantage of CareerBuilder.com's easy job postings, 10 million-plus résumés, comprehensive screening tools, and more. Millions of job seekers visit the site every month to search for opportunities, sign up for automatic e-mail job alerts, and get advice on job hunting and career management."

- **www.seniorjobbank.com/:** is a website specific to seniors. "The Job Site for Seniors: 100% Free to Over-50 Job Seekers. Completely confidential service matching job seekers over 50 with employers and good jobs."

- **Job search websites:** These may give you some leads, they are free, and you can navigate them at any time during the day.

- **Search engines (e.g., www.google.com, www.msn.com):** Use search engines to explore an industry of interest to you. You will be able to harvest the names of companies in that industry and trade publications, in addition to background information and new items on current events in that industry.

- **Company specific websites:** Once you have identified a specific company, go to its website. There is probably a link labeled "*Careers*" or "*Employment Opportunities.*" Remember to look at all jobs of interest.

- **Trade associations:** Many professions have an association of some kind. These days, they probably have a website. The website is a good source of information about the profession and may include a chat group. In addition, there may be a section with job listings.

- **Job fairs and open houses:** Job fairs are a good way to connect with a number of companies under one roof, including companies that you hadn't thought to consider before. They are a chance to meet company representatives face-to-face and let them know you as the person behind the résumé. An open house has many of the same benefits, but it is sponsored by one company and is held on their own premises. Job fairs are often advertised in the general press, as well as the trade press. You can also find information by searching for job fairs on a search engine like www.google.com.

- **Trade press:** There is at least one trade journal for most professions. They are a good source of general information, often include the names of companies in the feature stories, and may have a section of "positions available" advertisements.

- **AARP website (www.aarp.org):** AARP has a link for companies that have expressed a specific interest in hiring older Americans.

JOB FAIRS AND OPEN HOUSES

Here are some helpful hints for making the most out of job fairs and open houses:

- **Do attend:** You will be investing a small amount of your time that is likely to yield a significant number of contacts. Also, since you will be meeting people in person, you may get some useful feedback.

- **Dress appropriately:** You will look and feel more professional if you wear business attire. In general, a suit and tie for men and a dress or pants suit for women would help you create a positive first impression.

- **Introduce yourself properly:** For example, greet the company representative with a firm handshake. Say something, such as "Hello, my name is John Greene. I am interested in learning more about career opportunities with your company." If true, you could add, "I am especially interested in _____ opportunities," and/or "I am familiar with your company from my current job (or " . . . from reading your website after I found out that you would be at the job fair today").
- **Ask questions:** Don't just drop off your résumé. Talk with the company representative. Have some good questions ready, such as:
  - To what extent are teamwork, communication, and good judgment important to your company?
  - What can you tell me about the working environment at your company?
  - Why did you choose to work with this company?
- **Ask for business cards:** Ask for a business card so you will have contact information for the person you met.
- **Follow up:** Write a brief e-mail or letter to the representative of each company that interested you. About one week later, call those people. You will probably get their voice mail. That is all right. Your letter and subsequent call will increase the possibility of your getting a job interview because you have demonstrated a degree of interest, professionalism, and perseverance.

Here is a sample follow up e-mail after a job fair (a hard copy letter would be very similar):

(continued)

Ms. Jean Jones

Dear Ms. Jones:

It was a pleasure meeting with you at Middle Management Mavens Job Fair in the Hilton Hotel on April 3. I enjoyed our discussion about career opportunities for writers at [name of company]. I am interested in pursuing the possibility of a position with (name of company). For your convenience, I have attached another copy of my résumé.

Next week, I will call you to discuss what our next step should be.

Sincerely yours,

Lauren Fountain

4. Landing the Job

Going Online

Let's look at a hypothetical case. Rhonda is 60 years old. After working for 35 years, she retired early from teaching junior high school. Unfortunately, her husband has died. He hadn't carried a significant life insurance policy, he didn't have much of a pension, and their savings were minimal. Rhonda is going back to work. Let's assume that Rhonda is looking for a full-time, salaried job, and strongly prefers not to reenter her previous field.

This is what Rhonda did. She decided to start looking for opportunities using an online job posting site. In this case, she happened to start with America's JobBank (www.ajb.dni.us/), using the computer in her local library. Rhonda didn't yet have an account, so she supplied some basic information and then chose a username and password (which she of course wrote down for future reference). Then she was asked to choose an approach for searching the database. Rhonda could have chosen keyword or job title, but she chose to take a broader approach by clicking on "search all job categories" and supplying the name of her town and state. The system then searched within a 50-mile radius of that town.

Rhonda looked at the list of posted jobs. One that caught her eye was a case manager position in a group home. She had the requisite skills, although not the preferred degree. "That's all right," Rhonda said to herself. "I am interested, so I will apply. The worse that can happen is that they won't interview me." Rhonda could have applied by several methods. She could have pasted her résumé on to the system, including her cover letter as a preface to her résumé. However, she decided to utilize the e-mail option. She made note of the exact e-mail address. When Rhonda got home she accessed her e-mail account. In her e-mail, Rhonda included a cover letter, modified for this specific situation, with her résumé attached. She also made a note to herself to call the e-mail recipient the following week.

Pursuing a Specific Company

Jeannine identified several companies in her area that were of interest. One of those companies was Wonderco, a medium-sized company that specialized in property insurance. Jeannine went online and discovered that there were several customer service positions available. She applied directly online using the company's template as a vehicle to submit her résumé. However, Jeannine didn't leave it at that. She found on the website the name of the manager of customer service. (No e-mail address was given, but that was no problem. Jeannine simply requested it when she called Wonderco's main number.) Jeannine wrote a nice e-mail to the manager explaining that she was interested in a customer service position and wanted to let the manager know it, even though she had also applied online. Jeannine also asked a friend who worked at Wonderco to send a brief e-mail to that manager supporting Jeannine's application. The result of this extra effort was that the company proactively retrieved Jeannine's résumé from their database.

Taking the Initiative

David was also looking for a job, and his job search illustrates an important fact. You don't have to wait until you become aware of a job opening. David had been in the building trade and was just too worn out by age 58 to continue. Through his networking, he had gleaned an interesting idea: David could check out opportunities with companies that could use his building trade skills in a capacity that was less physically demanding. In his area was a company called Prime Building Suppliers, Inc. David looked up their website. It so happened that no jobs of interest to him were posted, but that didn't stop him. David wrote an e-mail to the company's vice president of operations (the name was easy to acquire from the website and it could have been acquired by simply calling the company's main telephone number). In his e-mail, David expressed his reasons for interest in the company and indicated his interest in exploring career possibilities or perhaps becoming an assistant manager in the distribution center. David made sure to be explicit about the skills and product knowledge he offered, in addition to his comfort level with the building culture and his contacts in the field. Although the vice president had nothing current to offer, he invited David to come in for an exploratory discussion. Three months later, a position opened up, and it was offered to David.

In each of these three examples, people applied for a job electronically. That is the most common practice today. However, there will be times when a hard copy cover letter and résumé will be requested. The thought process is largely the same. That said, it is a good idea to get comfortable with electronic submission of résumés.

Sometimes you will be interested in a company but cannot identify a specific job description from their website that appeals to you. That's all right. Take the initiative in your own hands. Write to the most senior person in the functional area of interest to you. Your letter might look like this:

44 Oakdale Street
Philadelphia , PA 19152

November 16, 2005

Ms. Jane Goodnaw
Vice President, Marketing
Widget Company
9500 Bustleton Avenue
Philadelphia, PA 19158

Dear Ms. Goodnaw:

Your name was recently mentioned in the *Philadelphia Inquirer* in connection with Widget Company's new home air purifying system. The article mentioned that the biggest challenge your company faces is marketing your unique concept with its premium price.

Based on my years of experience in home product sales, I have several marketing ideas that I would like to share with you. My résumé is enclosed to give some more information about my professional background.

Next week, I will call you to see if a meeting can be arranged at your convenience.

Sincerely,

Martin Greenwood
Encl.

Note a few things about the above letter.

1. Although the letter above is formatted as a hard copy letter, it is perfectly fine to send a letter of this type by e-mail. You can often acquire someone's business e-mail address simply by calling the company's main telephone number or by sending an e-mail requesting that information to the "contact us" or "information" function on their website. Also, you can see how those e-mail addresses that are given are structured. For example, if one is: first name.last name@company.com, Jane Goodnaw's address is probably Jane.Goodnaw@Widget.com.

2. When you call Jane Goodnaw, you may be asked by a receptionist if your call is about a job interview. You have every right to say that your call is in reference to your letter of November 16.

3. Remember that not every letter of this type will result in a meeting. Nevertheless, it is one more approach that you can try.

KIOSKS

Do you remember those paper applications we had to fill out when applying for a clerical job in an office or a cashier in a retail store? The good news is that, in large measure, they have disappeared. However, they have been replaced by job application kiosks. Here are some things you should know in advance, based on a trial run I conducted as a would-be applicant at a large retail store.

There were two desks near the customer service counter. Each was set up so that people could apply for a job. Instead of using pen and paper, the applicant uses a keyboard and computer. In this case at least, there was no mouse, only the keyboard to master. There was a diagram indicating which keys were for which function, but it took me a few minutes—and a tip from an employee—about how to use them to complete the five sections of the application.

The computer screens assure the user that the company complies with privacy standards and EEO requirements; therefore, I felt relatively comfortable supplying my social security number and address. A computer screen also informed me that an outside vendor might be used to compute and process my answers. I was informed by another screen that the company might check on my credit reports, criminal record, motor vehicle record, and similar matters. (It is not uncommon for employers

(continued)

to check those things, but it was a bit eerie being so advised by a computer in a local mall.) Then I was asked about educational history and work history, much in the manner that a paper application might.

The next section asked about preferred working hours, availability to work evenings and weekends, and anticipated hourly wage.

There was only one section you might not anticipate. There were 60 multiple-choice questions that the applicant was asked to answer based on their initial feeling. These questions asked my opinion about honesty in others, optimism, and what should be done in various situations that are likely to occur in this type of work environment (e.g., a store). I was assured that the store manager would not see my specific answers to these questions. However, they do form a key basis for a coded designation that will tell the manager what kind of questions she or he should ask if you are interviewed.

Nice features: At this kiosk, you could choose to answer the question in either English or Spanish. Also, you don't have to finish the entire application in one sitting. It is possible to complete the application by the end of the next business day. If you have a disability, you may ask a store employee to help you with the application, based on the ADA notion of "reasonable accommodation." If a required answer was skipped, the computer stopped you from going forward until the requisite information was supplied. Since your answers are entered by keystroke, your handwriting isn't going to be an issue.

Some suggestions:

- The computer screen told me that the application would take from 20 minutes to one hour to complete. Based on my experience, I suggest that you be prepared to spend more time than that.

- One question asked me to identify *one* job title of interest to me from over a dozen titles listed. I had no idea what some of the titles meant. There is a statement on the screen that all the available descriptions could be discussed at an interview, but I don't like to answer in the dark. I recommend asking at the customer service counter to read one or two job descriptions of possible interest. (At this store, there was no book of all the job descriptions available.)

- The section with the 60 questions (each with at least five possible answers) posed some pragmatic problems. First, it can be a strain on the eyes. Second, it can be a strain on your patience. If either your eyesight or your patience begins to fail, end that session and come back to it later.

- The questions about hoped-for hourly wage and working hours were among the few that could be skipped at this kiosk. You might want to leave those questions for a job interview if you are uncomfortable or uncertain about what to say at that point.

- If you have a mechanical problem, ask for assistance at the customer service desk. They are likely to help. However, the store employees will not explain a question or define a word you might not understand.

- Be sure to exit the application before leaving the kiosk. You do this simply by pressing the "ESC" (escape) key.

- Don't be surprised if the manager on duty is 20 to 40 years younger than you are.

(continued)

In the case of this kiosk, there was a red phone next to the computer. You are asked to pick it up and tell a store employee when you have finished. Apparently, the main purpose is to find out if you are applying for a position they are eager to fill. If you are, you might be invited to interview on the spot. For that reason, it makes sense to come to the kiosk in casual business attire.

There are two common enemies in a job search: discouragement and complacency.

Here is what you can do to fight *discouragement:*

- **Add irons to the fire:** Make applying for jobs part of your weekly routine. When you know that you have additional employers considering your résumé, bad news (or no news) about any given employment opportunity will feel less significant.
- **Continue pursuing informational interviews:** They are easier to arrange than job interviews, and they keep you actively involved with people in the field. What's more, you gain additional insights and may develop some job leads.
- **Be realistic from the outset**: You are likely to get many negative responses (or no response at all) before you hear the words "We want to offer you a job." But you will get to that point if you keep trying, and you only need one job at a time.

Complacency can also take the steam out of your job search. "I have a job interview next week" is not an invitation to stop looking for more job interviews. Remember this:

- You may feel less anxious at your job interview if you know that you don't have everything riding on it.
- An interview is not a job offer.
- If you develop more than one job offer, you will have a better chance to accept a job you really want. You are also in a position to negotiate better terms (e.g., a higher salary).

Some Helpful Hints

1. Follow Up

Don't forget to follow through properly. One way to do this is to set up a chart so that you can track the progress of each résumé you submit. For example:

Name of Company
Great Opportunity, Inc

Submitted Résumé
March 1

Action to Date
March 8: Called Harry Goodman at (603) 256-0986
(Left message on voice mail)

Next step
Call again on (date, two weeks from now)

Once you have submitted a résumé, it is a good idea to call about one week later to ask about your status (unless there is an explicit request for no phone calls). You will probably get a nondescript response at best, but that is OK. The point is that when you inquire in a polite professional way, you are showing more than average interest. That is a plus.

2. Include Smaller Companies in Your Job Search

Smaller companies account for about half of the total employment in the United States. Why ignore them? Smaller companies often care more about their employees as people, partly because the

Looking for a new job when you have left your last one involuntarily can be especially stressful. You may even be feeling a sense of rage and betrayal. Denise Snodgrass of the Center for Creative Retirement at the University of North Carolina makes these recommendations:

- Identify ways that you have dealt successfully with a crisis in the past. What has worked for you before is likely to work for you again.
- Share your story with others. Finding out that you are not alone in this situation is often helpful in itself.
- Take control of your situation and avoid self-pity. Look at what you want to do next. Do you want a similar job with another employer? Perhaps you want to consider doing something completely different, like a new career. The key is to identify what you want to do and what is necessary to pursue it.

managers and/or owners are apt to see them on a daily basis and may even live in the same community. In addition, smaller companies often offer the opportunity for broader, more varied tasks that may have a greater impact on the company. That may make your workweek more enjoyable.

3. Don't Shoot Yourself in the Foot

There are a number of ways you can hurt yourself. Here is a list of things to avoid:

- **Don't get hung up with thoughts about ageism, i.e., discrimination against older people based on their age:** This advice may seem counterintuitive. In a survey reported by the AARP in 2003, fully two-thirds of respondents believed that workers face age discrimination in the workplace today. Some men went so far as to undergo cosmetic surgery in order to look younger. Similarly, about 60 percent of respondents believed that older workers would be the first to go in a downsizing. (*AARP Staying ahead of the Curve*). Despite those common perceptions, I suggest you put thoughts of ageism out of your mind. To the extent that it does exist as a pure prejudice, there is not much you as an individual can do about it. Besides, age prejudice as such is not nearly as prevalent as many people believe. In fact, in 2002, the unemployment rate for people over the age of 50 was 3.9 percent, according to the Bureau of Labor Statistics. That was far less than the national average. *Lesson: If you are interested in a job, apply. Don't let fear of discrimination stand in your way. Otherwise fear of age as a barrier can become self-fulfilling.*
- **Don't read hostile intent into a job description:** If you are interested in a job, apply for it. Some older people assume

that terms like "energy," "fast-paced," or "fresh thinking" in a job posting are code words for "only young people need apply." If you indeed have energy and can offer fresh thinking, why not apply?

- **Don't assume that the world owes you something:** Yes, you have worked hard and sacrificed. You may have been a military veteran and a pillar of your community. But employers want to know what you can do for their company. In that regard, your past is a predictor that works in your favor, but it is not an "I Owe You."

- **Don't focus on what you are giving up or what you once had:** Focus on the positive aspects of a new job, like income, social contact, utilizing skills, etc. Otherwise, you are likely to carry a negative attitude into a job interview, a prime ingredient of interview failure.

In chapter 6 you learned how to build a winning strategy for your next job. In chapter 7 we will learn how to write a résumé that wins interviews.

Résumés for the Not Retired

OUR RÉSUMÉ is an honest commercial that says to a potential employer: "You really should interview me because I have the skills and attributes you need." Entire books have been written about this subject, but we will identify the main points in this chapter.

You can think of your résumé as having four basic parts.

1. **Summary:** A summary is a short statement of what you can give your next employer followed by a short statement indicating what type of job you are seeking. Your summary will be two or three sentences long. I recommend the term summary because it seems to encourage people to emphasize what they offer. The commonly used term "objective" often induces people to emphasize only what they want to get. When contacting a prospective employer, it is better to give than to receive.

2. **Experience Section:** This section will probably focus on paid work, but it could include volunteer work as well. It will be organized logically but not necessarily chronologically. This will not be a string of job descriptions. Instead, you will focus on skills and attributes that you have demonstrated and the results that you achieved.

3. **Education Section:** Typically this section will be relatively short. You will list the degrees you earned, generally putting the most recent or most advanced degree first. Listing your major field of study is often desirable. The date the degree was conferred is *optional* and older people are often best advised to leave the date out.

4. **Other Selling Points (OSPs):** This would include language skills, computer skills, related licenses and certifications, and honors received on the job or from civic groups. Where you list various OSPs on your résumé depends on how important they would be to your next prospective employer.

Here are the basic guidelines for seniors over the age of 55 writing their résumé:

General Rules

- **Don't rely on your existing résumé or simply build on it**: Your current résumé is probably more of a job description reflecting the past than a commercial for your *next* job. By starting fresh, you can design a résumé that better matches the needs of your next employer. After you have drafted a new résumé, use your current résumé as a check to make sure that you haven't forgotten anything of importance to your next job.

- **Don't lie or even mislead**: You know that *misleading* is the moral equivalent of *lying*, so there is no need to go into the matter of ethics here. The truth about you is stronger than any lie you could concoct. The truth just requires more of your time and energy to identify. For example, Arnie might be tempted to inflate a sales achievement by writing, "Increased widget sales by 25 percent annually." However, the truth may be even more impressive, "Increased widget sales by 10 percent annually—double the industry average." Likewise, the fact of being truthful is often a selling point in itself. Nobody is perfect. In fact, people who walk on water often leave puddles. On the other hand, everybody can be honest, and that is usually an irreducible criterion. Finally, misleading information can be disastrous for your career. If an experienced résumé reader feels that something is just not quite up front about your résumé, you are much less likely to be interviewed. If you *are* interviewed, and it is found that your résumé was misleading, you will probably not be offered the job even if you are a strong candidate in other areas. If you fool the interviewers, but the employer subsequently discovers that your résumé was untruthful, you can be fired summarily. Bottom line: if you need a lawyer to defend your résumé or a philosopher to explain it, rewrite your résumé.

Getting Started

- **Show your past and present as predictors for your future:** Your résumé should say to the employer, "I have done (or am doing) certain things. Therefore, there is a good probability that I would show those skills or produce similar results in the future. Based on that probability, it is worth your time to interview me." Therefore, your goal is to present the salient facts (namely skills, attributes, results achieved) in your professional (or volunteer) experience in terms that address what *your next* employer needs.

- **Identify what the job requires in terms of specific skills:** This is easiest if you have a specific job description. Lacking that, examine a cognate description for a similar job. Then review your skills inventory. Now you can match those skills and attributes the employer wants with the skills and attributes you offer.

- **Feature your prominent points:** Since your résumé will be read quickly, you want to write your résumé so that the most important points are prominent and therefore easily read. Here is your rule of thumb: if something is important, allocate more space to it. Also, the most important points should come early in your résumé.

Your summary conveys the essence of your message quickly. Let's say that you have industry knowledge, functional expertise, or established relationships that would benefit your next employer. All of these would be solid selling points. You could start building your summary with:

Summary: Finance professional with technical experience and established relationships in the widget industry . . .

Based on skills the job requires and that you have, you can write a second sentence. For example:

. . . Excellent analytical, research, and writing skills.

As a final step, you may add a short statement that links your professional goal with the company's need:

. . . Seeks to contribute financial expertise to a company in the tool manufacturing industry.

In this case, the summary now reads:

Summary: Finance professional with experience in the widget industry. Excellent analytical, research, and writing skills. Seeks to contribute financial expertise to a company in the tool manufacturing industry.

A bit later, we will also show how you might use your summary to explain gaps in your experience section.

Experience Section

- **Coordinate the experience section with your summary:** For example, if your summary cites analytical, research, and writing skills, make sure that you have résumé sentences that start with analyzed, researched, and wrote.
- **Use effective verbs:** Each résumé sentence in the experience section starts with a verb. (The subject is implied.) The verb should convey a skill you have demonstrated. For example, if you conducted surveys, start with "Surveyed." Don't start with "conducted" unless you want to conduct an orchestra or conduct electricity.
- **Show results:** A résumé sentence including the phrase "saved $10,000," or "reduced lead time by 10 percent," or "increased client base from 50 to 130" is a powerful selling point. Every prospective employer understands the importance of results. Quantifying your results when possible is even better.
- **Avoid useless words:** Adverbs tend to be useless. What is the point of writing "successfully"? No one would ever write unsuccessfully. Why say "currently developing," when "developing" conveys the same meaning?
- **Minimize age-related facts:** Don't hide your age, but you don't want to emphasize it either. In that respect, there is no

need to state the year of your college or high school graduation. That would be giving away your age, and you want age
to be a nonfactor. Also, you may want to skip some immediate posteducation work experiences. Unless you are
responding to a job description or help wanted ad that spec-
ifies a specific number of years of experience, avoid stating
that type of number. Even then, if the description calls for
some years of experience, you can say "over 10 years of experience," rather than "25 years of experience."

- **Avoid gap traps:** Gaps in your résumé raise the question of
  "where were you?" or "what happened?" At an interview, you
  may be able to address these issues satisfactorily. At the
  résumé stage, you don't want those questions raised in the
  employer's mind. You are not there to answer them, and
  doubt tends to discourage invitations to interviews. So what
  should you do about dates of employment?

This is what you should do: For periods of employment, put years
only, and exclude months.

Example one:
Job Y, 1999–2005
Job X, 1996–1999

is better than

Example two:
Job Y, October 1999–March, 2005
Job X, April, 1996–February, 1999

Example one doesn't raise the question, "What happened to the
applicant at Job X?" However, example two raises that question at

a glance. Example one also covers you for the entire year of 2005 (Job Y). As a secondary benefit, example one is also shorter and easier to read.

Here is an alternate solution: explain the gap explicitly on your résumé. You can do this in your summary. For example, Harry hasn't had a paying job at all for seven months. He can write "Seeks to continue career in the widget industry after accepting early retirement package from previous employer." Similarly, Judy may account for years spent between jobs in family raising: "From 1994 to 2004, stayed home to raise family" or "1992 to 2005 worked part-time in nonprofessional capacity while raising family."

Martha might make a different kind of statement to reflect her situation: "Relocated to San Diego area as trailing spouse. Seeks to continue career in biological research." Sam, who was laid off in a general company downsizing, could write: "Seeks to resume career after losing position in a company-wide layoff of 950 employees."

Statements of this type let people know that you are in transition, but that you were not *fired for cause* from your previous position. It is certainly true that the statements Harry and Martha are making should be included in a cover letter as well. However, there are many situations, such as job fairs, where there is no cover letter. Further, addressing the issue up front conveys a sense of openness and honesty.

You can also use your experience section for your transition statements. For example, Sam could write, "Lost position in a general downsizing of 950 employees" at the end of his text describing the skills and attributes he demonstrated at that job. Beth could write, "Temporarily left workforce to care for family" as the first line in her experience section if it explains a prolonged gap since her last job.

In any event, it often makes sense to put the dates of your employment where they are not conspicuous. I recommend putting dates at the end of the text associated with each job if the dates are potentially problematic.

The experience section must be logical but not necessarily chronological. The experience section should discuss first your most *related* work or volunteer experience but not necessarily your most *recent*. You may divide your experience into two or more subheadings, putting the *most important* first.

For example, let's say that you are applying to a company in the mattress industry. Your most recent experience was in airplane engines, but prior to that you had solid experience in consumer products. You could have two subheadings under professional experience: (1) consumer products and (2) industrial goods.

The sample résumés later in this chapter will show you examples of this structure.

This structure is honest and draws a connection between the employer's line of business and your experience. This type of structure is often called a *category résumé*. Along similar lines, if your stronger selling point is functional expertise, you could have two subheadings under experience: (1) marketing management and (2) sales.

Further Tips

- **Speak in the language of your next employer:** Avoid using terminology that has specific meaning to your current or most recent employer unless it also has meaning to your next employer. Breaking this rule is harmful to anyone, but for seniors it can be fatal. You do not want to convey the impression that you are so immersed in your past that you will be unable (or unwilling) to adjust to a new situation. Acronyms specific to your old company can be especially harmful.

- **Avoid long historical records:** The main purpose of your résumé is to get you invited to an interview in an honest manner. It is to your interest to focus on that instrumental fact. Many older people feel that they have to justify their lifetime of work (or absence from work) to the world. That is not so. You simply need to present yourself as a good match for the job you want next. Leave the emotional catharsis and historical record to your diary or family album.

- **Focus on less is more:** Brevity can be very difficult. *Don't expect to get it right the first time.* A good résumé will go through a number of writing iterations. *You are not trying to validate the past.* Your goal is to provide a predictor for your future performance. *Think about a typical commercial:* it shouldn't take time for the résumé reader to grasp what you want to say. An effective message can be relatively brief. Would you be attracted to a commercial that takes forever to get through (or a political candidate who drones on forever while saying very little of interest to you)? Of course, it takes more time to write concisely than to write loosely, but it is time well spent.

- **Match the needs of the job, don't overwhelm them:** Just give your next potential employer the facts. *This is especially true if you anticipate that your next job should be less stressful or demanding than your last one.* Employers are not looking for the most qualified person in the world, whatever that would mean. Therefore, they are not looking for the most impressive résumé in the world, whatever *that* would mean. Instead, employers are looking for a good match for the job at hand. One good way to approach this is to focus on your function, rather than the scope of your authority. For example, you can mention what skills you utilized and/or what you achieved without mentioning how many employees you managed. Also, through judicious use of graphics, you can de-emphasize job titles. Emphasizing titles makes it appear that you may still be a big fish who just won't fit in to a less august pond.

- **Anticipate and address unstated objections:** There are some widely held, but seldom-stated reservations about older job seekers. You can address them in your résumé. *This is especially important if you are seeking a position at your current (or even greater) level of responsibility.*

  - **Stuck in the mud:** Show growth through progression of titles or explicit statements (e.g., assumed broader responsibility for . . .).

  - **Not adaptive:** Indicate new methodologies or new technologies that you have mastered for the job. For example, *Evaluated proposals for outsourcing routine functions. Determined that savings would be short-term only. Recommended improved technology and some assignment changes, resulting in greater cost savings and enhanced morale.*

  - **Just wants to coast:** Show challenges tackled and assignments for which you volunteered. Also, you could use your most recent manager's opinion with a statement like this: *Praised in most recent annual review for dedication, energy, and good judgment.*

  - **Won't fit in:** Show that you are a team player. Include your work with more junior (i.e., younger) colleagues. Identify your mentoring role. You could write something like this: *Worked on teams that included both new and veteran employees to identify cost saving ideas for our unit. Mentored junior colleagues on communication skills and exercising professional judgment.*

Standard résumé advice makes sense if your goal is to make a lateral move or to move ahead. What should you do if you want to downshift to a position that is less demanding or to change to a completely different line of work?

There are two things you can do with your résumé:

- Use your summary for that purpose. You might say: "Seeks to apply my interpersonal skills and organizational strengths in a... (customer service, peer counseling, supervisory capacity)" or "Goal is to continue manufacturing career in a standard 40-hour day-shift environment."
- Organize your experience section in two subheadings. The first will be skills and attributes, and the second will be a simple list of your employers and titles.

In addition, use the first paragraph of your cover letter to state explicitly that you have decided to make a change at this point in your life and to contribute your talents in a different function or a different environment.

Draft a New Résumé

You have already developed a skills inventory (chapter 6). Now find a description of a job you may want to pursue. You could find examples by looking on job search websites or the career links of companies that might employ people for positions such as yours. Companies that are similar to a company of interest to you can be a useful source. Let's say that you are interested in the mutual fund industry. Many of the positions that people hold at, let's say,

Fidelity Investments, will be similar to those at another mutual fund company, like Vanguard.

It would be impossible to include a sample résumé for each possible situation a reader may encounter. However the samples given here should be enough to give you some good ideas.

The first résumé is for Lauren Smithfield, a woman who took time out from her career to raise a family. Lauren has some recent temp experience and now wants to apply for a more professional level job. Notice that Lauren mentions that her family-raising responsibilities are in the past. That helps her explain the gaps in her paid employment while also indicating that child rearing is no longer an issue for her. Also, Lauren has utilized the *category* format in her experience section. In that way she can highlight that she has at least some of the experience her hoped-for next employer would want. In addition, she is able to show leadership capabilities, albeit in a voluntary setting. Notice that Lauren has wisely de-emphasized dates. They are at the end of each blurb in her experience section and entirely missing from her education section. It is quite possible that Lauren worked at one or more jobs after college that she has chosen not to include. Everything you write must be true, but you don't have to write everything.

LAUREN SMITHFIELD
93 Devonshire Drive
Happy Valley, MI 48109
(616) 584-9854
laurensmithfield@aol.com

Summary: Planning, organization, and communication skills. Proven leader; goal-oriented but flexible. Returning to workforce after time-out to finish raising my family. Seeks administrative position in a physicians' practice group.

ADMINISTRATIVE EXPERIENCE
Very Good Product, Inc. Grand Rapids, MI
Excellent Eateries Lower Falls, MI
Demonstrated flexibility by moving among six different function areas to substitute for vacationing employees. Responded to customer inquiries and built files on Excel and Access. Developed basic financial reports using Lotus. Learned about specific business concerns in office supply and prepared food industries. Positions were long-term temporary assignments. (2003–2005)

MANAGEMENT EXPERIENCE
Vice President, Singing for At-Risk Children (SARC)
Detroit, MI
Planned annual conference for individual and corporate sponsors. Organized concert tours for at-risk children served by foundation. Spoke to civic gatherings and media to publicize SARC. Complied with government regulations and detailed bylaws while building 600-client organization. Promoted four times in three years. (1990–1993)

LEADERSHIP EXPERIENCE

Vice President, PTO Happy Valley, MI

Directed fund-raising campaign involving 20 volunteers that yielded $250,000 in labor, materials, and cash for a new recreational facility. Persuaded local merchants to donate material in exchange for goodwill. Researched fund-raising techniques using the Internet. Created Access file of contributors. (1996–1998)

President, Royal Bear Civic Association Grand Rapids, MI

Elected because of excellent management and leadership skills. (1992–1994)

EDUCATION

Escola College, Meriden, CT

Bachelor of Arts

Major: Communications; graduated *cum laude*

Computer Skills: Access, Excel, Lotus

Robert Franklin wants to stress that he is a marketing professional. Therefore, he uses bold for his titles, but not for his specific employers. Robert's résumé is chronological in style. However, he emphasizes that he is a marketing professional by referring specifically to marketing experience. Robert does not consider it a selling point to discuss any positions he may have held prior to starting on this career path. Robert has been a bit creative by including laudatory comments others have made about him early in his résumé. Further, he has divided each employment experience into accomplishments and responsibilities. This is not a bad approach, especially for someone seeking a high-level position. In this circumstance, there is also no need for Robert to worry that his résumé is two pages rather than one. However, he wants to make sure that the most important, compelling presentation is on page one.

ROBERT FRANKLIN
293 Wildflower Drive
Minneapolis, MN 55402
(612) 973-1256 (H)
(612) 584-4121
E-mail: rfranklin@aol.com

*"His creativity is matched by his skill in precise implementation.
Robert has enabled us to cut the lead time in bringing products
to market by six months." –2005 Annual Performance Review*

*"Robert has been a critical factor in returning our division to
profitability." –William Tiller, vice president of Widget Home
Appliance Division*

MARKETING EXPERIENCE

Consumer Delight Corporation   Austin, TX
Manager of Planning   (2002–present)
*Four years of increasing responsibilities with this $600 million
consumer products company.*
ACHIEVEMENTS:

- Inaugurated Tough Toe Nail line; added $20 million
  annually to the bottom line which added $20 million
  annually to company's profit
- Reduced product design and advertising costs by
  $2 million (15 percent) using PIMS
- Integrated teams of marketing, finance, and logistics staff
  that accelerated introduction of products to market
- Developed contingency plan to deal with possibility of
  stagnant economic growth

RESPONSIBILITIES:
- Determined new product lines consistent with company's strategic goals
- Forecasted future potential of current products
- Supervised staff of four analysts and two planners who track production and price points

Widget Corporation,   Dayton, OH
Home Appliance Division
Director of Forecasting   (1999–2002)
First marketing forecaster for this $500 million consumer durable product firm.
ACHIEVEMENTS:
- Forecasted demand by product and demographic segment; reduced need for production overtime by $200,000 (10 percent)
- Identified potential areas for product differentiation; resulted in repositioned midrange products
- Reduced unsold inventory by accurate analysis of cycles for main products

RESPONSIBILITIES:
- Analyzed microeconomic demographic and consumer data
- Monitored actual sales against previous forecasts
- Reported monthly to senior management with recommendations for changes in market strategies

Beautiful Basics, Inc.   . Windsor, CT
Senior Marketing Analyst   (1994–1999)
Promoted rapidly due to excellent analytical and interpersonal skills, which benefited this privately held pillow company

ACHIEVEMENTS:
- Identified data for predicting pillow purchases from sleep patterns
- Recommended optimal channels of distribution, reducing logistics costs
- Began as marketing assistant; promoted more quickly to current position than any predecessor in company

RESPONSIBILITIES:
- Researched primary and secondary sources to identify best reliable data available at minimum costs
- Managed "Secret Shopper" program
- Collected data and anecdotal evidence from sales force

EDUCATION
Bachelor of Business Administration
University of Massachusetts at Amherst
Major: Marketing; Minor: Statistics

Computer Skills – Internet for computer research; Excel, Markatel, Datacrunch.

Personal – Active in local chapters of American Marketing Association and National Sleep Tight organization.

Gabrielle Golden worked in the technical services industry prior to her company moving out of state. She wants to continue in that industry. Notice that Gabrielle does not need to write about all the jobs she has ever held. Instead she calls attention to those that are in the technical service industry. Gabrielle has allocated the most space to her most important job. That job is also listed first. This makes good sense as space and location are two indicators of importance in the eyes of a potential employer. Like Lauren, Gabrielle de-emphasizes dates. She does this by putting them at the end of her blurb in the technical service experience section and by omitting dates altogether elsewhere in her résumé. Gabrielle has also chosen to explain why she is not currently working. That can be a very good idea since the cause was obviously beyond her control.

Gabrielle has decided not to have a full summary because she has formatted her experience section to show the relationship between her experience and her desired next job at a glance.

GABRIELLE GOLDEN
96 Holten Road
Bismarck, ND
(701) 247-9853
bgolden@yahoo.com

Career Goal: To continue a career in the technical service industry.

TECHNICAL SERVICE EXPERIENCE
Technical Service Manager
Laser Guided Production, Bismarck, ND
Provided customers throughout western U.S. with training and logistical support
- Trained installation and maintenance crews
- Responded to technical inquiries from client and sales staff
- Supervised installations for large clients
Position terminated when company moved out of state.
(1996–2005)

Service Technician
Computer Wizards, Inc., Fargo, ND
Repaired work station computers and LANs for this
$750 million high-tech manufacturer
- Praised by clients for excellent problem-solving skills
  and on-time service
- Praised by management for expertise and cooperation
  with other departments, especially marketing (1993–1996)

Production
Printing Palace, Inc., Chevy Chase, MD
Designed high-end printers and mass mailers. Awarded two
patents. (1988–1993)

OTHER WORK EXPERIENCE
Various technical and nontechnical positions following
military service.

MILITARY EXPERIENCE
United States Navy
Petty Officer Second Class
Fundamentals of submarine search; track and attack methods
Electronic maintenance specialist
Special training; radar theory; acoustic antisubmarine
    warfare; deployed in Keflank, Iceland, and Sigonella,
    Sicily
Honorable discharge; Navy Achievement Medal

EDUCATION
Certified for electronic and mechanical maintenance 2,000
hours: specialized equipment training; high school diploma

Computer Skills: JAVA, Scimpy, Html, C++

In this chapter you learned how to write a résumé that tells a prospective employer you have the skills that she or he wants. In chapter 8, we will look at your résumé's powerful partner, a good cover letter.

Cover Letters for the Middle-Aged and Beyond

N THE LAST chapter, we learned how to write an interview-winning résumé that overcomes problems that may be related to your age. In this chapter, we will learn how to write a cover letter that is your résumé's value-adding partner. We will look at two parts of writing a cover letter: (1) how your cover letter adds value and (2) the structure of a cover letter.

How Your Cover Letter Adds Value

Your cover letter provides an opportunity to augment your résumé in these ways:

- *Explain your motivation*: Your cover letter provides an opportunity to explain your motivation for wanting that *specific* job with that *specific* company.
- *Address "credibility gap" issues*: If the prospective employer looks at your résumé and spots any credibility issues, you

may have a problem. For example, you currently live in Pennsylvania, but you are applying for a job in North Carolina. In that case you should explain your connection to North Carolina. For example, you may want to move closer to family. If the reason is you are moving to a retirement community in North Carolina, you don't have to be that specific. All you need to say is that you are relocating. Suppose you have not had paid work experience for the past 10 years because you were at home caring for a family member. You could say so (while hopefully indicating how you have stayed current in some measure with the requisite skills to do the job). If you are returning to the workforce due to the death or disability of a spouse, you could say so. If you are uncomfortable with being explicit, simply say that you have experienced a change in family circumstances.

- *Add new material:* There may be one or more selling points you wish to convey that are relevant to a specific job opportunity but aren't on your résumé. Ideally, you would rewrite your résumé to reflect these selling points, but there are occasions when you just won't have the time. Similarly, you can use your cover letter to *highlight* items of particular importance to a specific employer that are not prominent or easily noticed on your résumé. You can also *reframe* items in a way that will connect them explicitly to the prospective employer's needs.

- *Indicate serious intent:* The very fact that you took the trouble to write a cover letter indicates a serious interest in the job. If you are applying electronically (e.g., e-mail, website), it may not be required and will therefore be all the more meaningful. If you are applying by hard copy through the U.S. mail, a cover letter is expected. In that case it will be the *quality* of your letter, rather than the very fact of writing it, which will make the difference.

Structure of Your Cover Letter

Your cover letter should be logically structured and business-like in tone. Each cover letter should be tailored to the *specific* job opportunity and company. All-purpose, generic cover letters that you could mass produce and send to just anybody are generally not effective. There should be four paragraphs:

First Paragraph (What I Am Writing About)

Identify your purpose in writing. If someone known to the recipient suggested you write, state that fact clearly in the first sentence. It may be a good idea to include his or her title if that would help grab the recipient's attention. Identify the position that you are writing about. You could have a one-sentence summary of your qualifications, such as, "My six years of applied experience in this field should make me an asset to your company." (If true, you could also say something like this: "I offer you everything your job description calls for and more.")

Second Paragraph (Why You Should Interview Me)

Indicate the benefits you bring to the company, namely, those qualifications the company needs that you have. Include a short example with each qualification. The style used in the Joseph illustration, which appears later, is easy to read and is also easy "to track" (i.e., to correlate the company's expressed *desiderata* with your qualifications). If you can offer even more than what the position requires, this is a good place to express it.

Third Paragraph (Why I Am Interested in Working For You)

State what it is about the specific job or type of job that you find appealing. Also, cite reasons why you want to work for *that company specifically*. It is easy to find nice things about the company on their own website. There is no harm telling an employer that you like something that they are obviously proud of as well. You may also want to express an interest in the profession generally or the industry of which the company is a part. Your statements in this paragraph will indicate whether you have done some basic research and if you are seriously interested in this specific opportunity. Be sincere, specific, *and don't write anything about the job or company unless you are certain that it is true.*

Fourth Paragraph (Closing and Next Step)

This is the place to mention your résumé. Refer to your résumé as "enclosed" in the case of hard copy. In an e-mail, your résumé will probably be "attached" but it might be "below" if the recipient has requested it that way. Make sure to state that it is *you* who will take the next step (i.e., you will contact the recipient the following week to see if a meeting can be arranged). An exception would be if you have strong reason to believe that the recipient doesn't want to be called on the telephone or that making a call would be impossible.

Checklist for a Cover Letter

Be sure to review this list before sending out each and every cover letter.

1. If your letter is hard copy, it should be produced on high quality paper. Also, make sure *to sign* your letter in blue or black ink. Your hard copy letter should include your return address, the full name, title, and address of the recipient and the date.
2. Whether your letter is hard copy or electronic, make sure that there are no spelling or grammatical errors. Using spell-check is useful but not sufficient for this purpose. Use

INCLUDE SALARY EXPECTATIONS?

More often than not, the best thing to do is to include a nondescript statement like "My salary expectations are reasonable and consistent with what is competitive in the market for a position of this nature." If you feel compelled to give a number, give a range, for example "My salary expectations are in the mid-$40s to mid-$50s." Is there some risk that a nondescript statement will hurt your chances of interviewing? Yes. However, if you give a number, it is likely to be too high or too low, so that could undermine your chances as well. Besides, would you want to work for a company that makes knowing your salary expectations a precondition for a job interview?

your eyeballs also. (Remember that 'manger' and 'manager' are both acceptable to an electronic spellchecker.) Use a dictionary if you have the slightest doubt about the proper spelling or usage of a word.

3. If you are sending an e-mail and have more than one account, use the one that utilizes your actual name rather than a moniker (e.g., Hotshot123) that doesn't lend itself to name recognition and may appear to be unprofessional.

4. In the subject line of your e-mail, indicate the title or reference number of the job you are seeking. If the position is available with that company in more than one geographic location, specify the name of the location you want as well.

Addressing the Employer's Needs in a Cover Letter

Let's look at a relatively straightforward case. You have read a "help wanted" notice or job description on a job-listing website like

Monster, on a specific company website, in a trade journal, or even your Sunday newspaper. In responding, whether by hard copy or electronically, your cover letter should address in a clear and easily visible way the characteristics the job description has indicated as desirable or necessary in prospective candidates.

Let's step outside of our day-to-day world for a few moments. Imagine that the Biblical Joseph spots the "help-wanted" notice in a newspaper. This position would be a career step up from the prison into which he has been tossed. He carefully reads what the potential employer (Pharaoh) wants in terms of skills and attributes from the person who will do this job. Then Joseph carefully crafts his cover letter accordingly.

Position Available: Seeking an interpreter of dreams. Must have a high sense of integrity and foresight. Education in a proverbial School of Hard Knocks highly desirable. Interested applicants should respond to: **The Senior Advisor, Pharaoh's Palace, Ancient Egypt.**

Sample cover letter in response to position available notice

Pit # 4
Prison
3,500 years ago

The Senior Advisor
Pharaoh's Palace
Ancient Egypt

Dear Mr. Senior Advisor: (That's how officials in those days would be addressed in cover letters.)

I was excited to read in the Palace Press that you are seeking an **Interpreter of Dreams for Pharaoh.** Let me tell you why I am the person you need:

Dream interpretation: Have been interpreting dreams since I was a youth. Although some are temporarily unfulfilled, my success rate in Egypt has been 100 percent.

Integrity: Refused the improper advances of Potiphar's wife even at my own peril.

Foresight: Realized the importance of storing grain during the seven years of plenty to feed people during the seven years of famine.

School of Hard Knocks: Have been cast into a pit by my brothers, sold into slavery, betrayed by my former boss's wife, and thrown into prison. Each has been a fruitful, albeit painful, learning experience.

Interpreting dreams for Pharaoh would be very appealing to me. It is a talent I enjoy utilizing, and I have enormous respect for a world leader who is like a god to his people. Also, relocating to the palace would pose no logistical problems for me.

It is several millennia too early for résumés, but your personal butler knows about my abilities and could render them to you orally. Next week I will contact your office in the palace to see if a meeting can be arranged at your convenience.

Sincerely,

Joseph Jacobson

This is what Joseph has accomplished in his cover letter:

- **Identified the job:** Joseph wrote in the first paragraph how he found out about it.
- **Addressed each of the qualities:** He responded to each quality the notice mentions in an easy-to-read manner.
- **Indicated his interest:** Joseph explains why he's interested in this position, including some praise for the prospective employer.
- **Overturned credibility gap issue:** Since Joseph is in prison, he turned his situation into a positive by indicating that relocation is not a problem. The reference to the butler serves a similar purpose.
- **Will follow up:** He states that he will do this the following week.

You may want to let people know that you are available without waiting for a job description to appear. For example, Celia lost her job as a marketing executive in a general downsizing. Of course she followed all the networking and job search advice that we gave in previous chapters. However, Celia didn't leave it at that. She identified companies within the scope of her geographical area that might be of interest. Then she wrote to the highest executive in that functional area. For example, she found that a company called Hometools was only a 45-minute commute. Checking online, she found that Arnold McAllister was the vice president for marketing. This is the hard copy letter that Celia wrote:

If you are responding to a job description, follow the directions for applying. For example, you may be asked to send your résumé by e-mail or to post it online. However, you can do *more* than the minimum that is requested:

- Before you post your résumé, add your cover letter to it as a preface. That way you will be posting a single document that includes the value added power of your cover letter.
- If you know someone in the company, let him or her know that you have applied for a job. I encourage you to include (attach) your résumé to your message. Many times a friend or colleague will then forward your material to the appropriate person with some words of recommendation.
- If you *don't* know somebody in the company, find someone who is in some way related to the job (e.g., the most senior officer for that function, a human resource manager, the CEO). Names can often be found on the company website. If e-mail addresses are not posted, they can often be obtained by calling the company's main number. Amend your cover letter by adding that you have also applied online for that position. Your purpose is to encourage someone to look at your application rather than hoping that your résumé will simply surface from the company's database on its own. At the worse, your additional letter will be ignored, so you have nothing to lose but a few minutes of your time.

1885 Goodweather Drive
Seattle, WA 98117

December 10, 2006

Mr. Arnold McAllister
Vice President, Marketing
Hometools, Inc.
Spaceneedle, WA 98197

Dear Mr. McAllister:

As one marketing professional to another, perhaps we can be of assistance to each other. I am looking for my next job, and you may need a successful product manager.

You probably want to know why I say "successful." Here are a few examples:

- I guided a new invention through a thicket of regulatory barriers and initial market indifference. Today the product is grossing $215 million per year.
- I managed a children's toy project from market research to distribution in the stores. Profits have been between $20 and $25 million for six years.
- I negotiated an advertising contract that purchased prime time at reduced rates. The product gained national recognition while advertising costs were 20 percent less than budgeted.

Marketing for me is more than a job—it is my passion. For that reason, I am being very selective in companies I contact. Hometools appeals to me because I admire the simple ingenuity of your products. As your CEO, Jeannine Champ, said, "We pick the best designs without picking the consumers' pockets."

If you think that there may be a match between your company and my talents, let's discuss it. I will call you next week to find out what your thoughts are.

Sincerely yours,
Celia Faunce

Your well-prepared strategy, your résumé, and your cover letter will open doors to job interviews. In chapter 9, we will learn how to ace your job interview.

Interviewing between 55 and 85: Age Can Be an Asset

OU HAVE probably gone to a job interview before. However, it may have been some time ago and under different circumstances. In this chapter, we will tell you how to land that next job.

There are two important steps in preparing for your interview: (1) preparing for the questions you will be asked (and the questions you will ask the interviewer) and (2) having the right attitude.

Let's simplify things a bit. There are hundreds of questions that could be asked at a job interview, but almost all of them fit into four major categories:

- Why should we hire you?
- Why do you want to work for us?
- What do you know about our company?
- Do you have any questions to ask me?

Let's take a look at each of these categories and construct some basic responses.

Why Should We Hire You?

"The reason you should hire me is that you need a person with certain attributes, and I have them." Now let's proceed with the details. Look at the job description, make a list of the skills and attributes needed, and then write at least one example demonstrating that you have that skill or attribute. You have already done something like this when you built your skills inventory. *It would be especially helpful for the older worker to have examples that are recent.*

Why Do You Want to Work for Us?

"I want to work for you because this job and this company are very appealing to me." There are two parts to this: the job and the company. Regarding the job, pick three or four aspects that are appealing to you based on the job description and indicate that you enjoy doing those things. Similarly, by reading the company's own website, including their recent press releases, you will know what the company is proud about. Pick three or four of those things and explain why they appeal to you.

Your motivation for wanting the job may be as important as the skill you would bring to it. Be sure that your motive is sincere, forward looking, and realistic in light of what the job offers. *If you are simply looking for a paycheck, you are less likely to get hired for a job that requires intrinsic motivation, energy, etc.*

If the position represents a downshift or a complete change, be honest about that as well: *"At this stage in my life I am looking for something meaningful but not as all consuming and stressful as my previous experiences."* or *" What I am looking for now is a position that allows me to be helpful to people on a one-to-one basis, and a retail store environment fits that goal perfectly.*" On the other hand, if the position represents a parallel move or a step up in responsibility, focus on how the position contributes to your long-term career goals.

What Do You Know about Our Company?

" *I have read your website and researched other sources online. (If true, you can add: "I have also checked some material in the library and spoken with some of your current and former employees.) Here is some of what I know.*" You should now be able to talk about:

- **Company's products and /or services:** What are the company's products and/or services? What are their key features? Who buys them?
- **Basic facts about the company's history:** When was it established and what is the significance (if any) of its name?
- **Company's rank in the industry:** Additionally, who are its major clients, customers, and competitors?
- **Recent news events involving the company:** You will often find a treasure trove of items in the media section of their website. Since these will probably be favorable items, they are a good source for your response to the company aspect of "Why do you want to work for us?" Of course, you should also be aware of more problematic new stories. Google.com and the website of major news organizations may be useful sources.
- **Company's special pride:** Is it their products, their employees, the way employees are treated, or recent achievements? Again, this information is very useful is preparing for the "Why do you want to work for us?" question.

- **Senior management description of company's performance:** This information is usually contained in the message to stockholders section in the company's annual report or on their website.
- **Challenges the company faces in the near future:** For older people, it is helpful to show that you are thinking about the future because you want to be a part of that future. This type of information may be found in the message to stockholders section, the general press (articles about pending legislation, economic conditions, political events at home or abroad), and the business/professional press. As you read these articles, think about the implications for the company you are trying to join.

Do You Have Any Questions to Ask Me?

"Yes, I do have some questions to ask you. Do you mind if I refer to my notes?" You should prepare at least five good questions to ask your interviewer. At least two should be about doing the job and two about the company. You might also ask about the industry in general or broader issues (e.g., consumer taste, new technologies) as they impact on the job and/or the company. Here are a few rules for preparing your questions:

- If you don't care, don't ask. Nothing is worse than being insincere.
- Your question should reflect the fact that you have read about and thought about the subject and would now like to know more.
- Don't let your questions erect barriers to your candidacy. For example, don't initiate a question like, "Is working late a requirement?" This question implies that you are out the door at 5 p.m., not exactly a selling point. "Would I have to

work with computers?" implies that you may have a weakness there. Not a selling point. Of course, if you are asked about limits on your working hours or your computer skills, give an honest answer.

■ Don't initiate a question about salary or benefits. From the perspective of both interview etiquette and pragmatics, it is better to have the interviewer raise this subject, if it is to be raised at all.

SAMPLE QUESTIONS YOU MIGHT ASK

Here are some questions that you might have ready to ask your interviewer:

QUESTIONS ABOUT THE JOB ITSELF

■ I read in the job description that teamwork is very important. Can you tell me if teamwork is an informal concept here, or are there formally organized teams? Does the company want people to represent the viewpoint of their specific department or to approach issues from a more company-wide perspective?

■ Researching databases is an important part of this job. What databases do you currently utilize, and how frequently are they updated? Have you found some databases to be more productive than others?

■ Before you were promoted, you held a position similar to the one for which I am interviewing. What did you find most challenging? Most rewarding? Looking back, was there anything that you would like to change?

(continued)

- If I do very well in the position we are discussing today, what would be a potential next career step for me with this company? (If you are looking just for a short-term job to make a few extra dollars or just something to occupy your time, this would not be a good question.)

The virtue in the first three questions is that you are demonstrating a serious interest in how the job is actually done. The fourth question indicates that you are looking for a serious job with promotional potential, not just a place to hang your hat.

QUESTIONS ABOUT THE COMPANY

- MSNBC reported that two of Yourco's competitors are planning to merge. The combined company would be larger than Yourco. Do you think that Yourco will need to revise its marketing approach, which is based on being "the leading company in the widget field"?
- Your website indicates that Productco manufactures a number of consumer products. How does the company manage to compete so successfully against products made in low-wage countries?

With questions like these, you demonstrate that you have enough interest to do some research about the company and that you are curious about issues that are important to people who are already employees.

QUESTIONS ABOUT THE INDUSTRY

- *Business Week* reported that some companies in this industry are outsourcing service functions so that they can focus on the company's core competencies. Do you think that this approach would be advantageous or disadvantageous to Thisco?

■ Because of public displeasure with questionable business practices, there is some movement toward more extensive governmental regulation of this industry. Is Thisco preparing for that possibility?

Questions like these show that you are thinking broadly about the industry as a whole and applying an industry-wide situation to the company's specific situation.

QUESTIONS ABOUT EXTERNAL FACTORS

■ When the price of gasoline goes up significantly, people tend to modify their driving habits, especially when it comes to long vacation trips. Touristco depends on tourists who come to the area by car. If the price of gasoline goes up another fifty cents per gallon, how will the company go about attracting tourists?

■ Snackco generates most of its revenue from its especially tasty snacks, which are high in sugar and calories. If there is a shift to more health-conscious eating, how will Snackco position its products?

Questions like these show that you are thinking about how factors beyond the company's control may have an impact. Senior managers tend to be concerned about things like that. These questions show one way in which your age and maturity could be an asset.

Identifying Job-Specific Questions

After you have done your preparation based on the four large categories noted above, you should identify job-specific questions you may be asked.

Required Skills and Attributes

Look at the job description and see what the requirements are, which you may have already done when you rewrote your résumé. Those skills and attributes will form the basis for most of the job-specific questions you will be asked. For example, let's say that *leadership* is mentioned in the job description. You may be asked a question like this: *"Think about a time when you exercised a leadership role. How did you become the leader? What challenges did you face? What did you achieve?"* If the job description mentions problem solving, prepare for a question like the following, *"Describe a problem you solved on your own and a problem you solved working with others."* Sometimes a skill or attribute is implied by the nature of the job. For example, dealing with people in tense circumstances is important to many jobs. You may be asked, *"Tell me about a situation in the past year when you had to deal with a very upset customer or coworker. How did you handle that situation?"* A skill like time management is another that may be implied rather than stated explicitly. Therefore you should expect a question like, *"How do you go about managing your time to accomplish your goals? How do you set priorities?"*

Reasons on Leaving Your Current Job

If you are now working, this is a reasonable question. The first step here is to say something nice about your current work situation. For example, *"I have been working for a wonderful company. I enjoy going to work, my colleagues, and the sense of satisfaction I gain from doing a job well."* Now you may proceed with the second step, a short statement about your current situation. *"Unfortunately, I have been caught in a downsizing,"* or *" The company is relocating, and I have decided not to uproot myself to follow it,"* or, *"There is new senior management, and they want new middle management. Along with some of my friends, I am being asked to leave,"* or *" I am now looking for a new position that will utilize my talent but will be less strenuous."* The third step is to transition to why you are interested in the job and company for which you are now interviewing. *"The reason I am so interested in your company is . . . "* You can now proceed with the answer you prepared for "Why do you want to work for us?"

Your Weaknesses

This type of question is not asked nearly as often as it once was, but you still need to be prepared for it. We are all human, so we all have some weaknesses. However, if you are asked this question, you must finesse an awkward situation. You will not win points by reciting a long list of shortcomings. On the other hand if you deny that you have any weaknesses at all, you may destroy your credibility. There are three things you can do. The first is to refer to a weakness that is really a strength. An example might be your determination to complete all your assignments by or before a deadline. (The interviewer will know that this is really a strength, not a weakness, but that is OK. You are not obligated to give information against yourself, especially when you have been asked a trick question.) The interviewer may proceed to ask for another weakness. In that case you may proceed to a second type of response by picking an attribute that is not essential to the job being discussed. For example, you might say, *"Although I am a good communicator in writing or in speaking to a small group, I do not feel comfortable speaking to a large group."* It would be a good idea to indicate how you are trying to remediate the weakness you mentioned, if that is true. If the interviewer proceeds along this line (which is unlikely) you may proceed with the third type of response. Express your openness to addressing any weakness of concern to the interviewer but ask if he or she could specify what potential weaknesses they would like you to discuss. For example, *"Everybody has their weaknesses, but I would like to address those skills or characteristics that are of interest to you. Is there anything about me that you would like to address?"*

Hypothetical Questions

The hypothetical question is not as common as it used to be, but you should be prepared just in case. There are three possible approaches. First, actualize the hypothetical, that is, talk about an actual situation. For example, *"I was in a situation like that one. Let me tell you how I handled it . . . "* This approach has the dual advantage of being easier for you to handle and more useful for the interviewer to evaluate. A second approach is to think in terms of the process you would follow to solve the problem: What would you need to know? What would your priorities be? What external interests would you have to consider? The question may raise a hypothetical situation that you would work hard to prevent. Then you could use a third approach, namely "It wouldn't happen because . . . " For example, *"I doubt that I would actually ever be pressed by two conflicting deadlines because I always plan ahead and put my ducks in a row long before a deadline looms. Let me give you an example . . . "*

Age-Related Questions

No trained interviewer will ask you how old you are. However, you may be asked questions reflecting concerns that are especially prevalent where older workers are concerned. This is actually to your advantage because a concern that is raised is a concern that can be allayed with a good answer. For example, if there is concern about your ability to deal with stress, you may be asked "Describe a time when you were faced with problems of stress at work that tested your coping skills. What was the cause of the stress, and what did you do?" There are several things to notice about this question. One is that the question has multiple parts (i.e., a time, cause, what you did). Second, if taken too literally, it may lead you to respond about the problem of stress, rather than simply stress *per se*. Third, it is implied, although not stated, that your response should refer to a reasonably recent situation.

Although it is impossible to construct a response that would apply to every reader, your answer could be something like this: *"Stress is part of my job, and I expect it. Last year, we had a large order from a good customer with an unexpected condition attached. We had to deliver the finished product in three months instead of the usual five. Senior management decided that there was too much money involved in this order to leave it on the table. So I was one of three people tasked with handling the increased burden on our supply chain. My specific responsibility was to assure that we could absorb the increased flow of materials into production without building up excess inventory or utilizing manufacturing overtime more than necessary. A supply chain is inherently stressful because there are many factors involved that must come together, yet I really don't control most of them. I deal with this stress by scoping out the nature of the problem and identifying the pieces of a possible solution. That way a huge task can be dealt with in smaller parts. What I did in this case was outline a possible plan of action right away and spoke with key players about it. Would you like me to go into greater detail?"*

Because this response addresses the three parts of the question, it is a bit longer than typical answers may be. When you feel that you may be straining the interviewer's listening ability a bit, it is a good idea to ask if she or he would like more details.

If there is concern about your degree of flexibility, you may be asked: "Can you tell me about a specific occasion when you conformed to a policy even though you didn't *agree with it?*" As with all questions, you must be careful not to reveal proprietary information about your current or past employer. You must also be careful not to bad-mouth an employer. (For example, if you said "Sure, we had plenty of dumb policies, but I liked my paycheck so I went along with them," you would be reflecting negatively on yourself and no one else). You might respond like this for the policies you dealt with that are too sensitive to discuss outside the company: *"Policies are made for a reason, even if I don't understand it or would prefer another policy. Our company is ABC Incorporated, not ME, Inc. That said, I have questioned the rationale or implications of policies, but I carry them out. Unfortunately, I cannot in good faith give you any specifics because the policies I carry out deal with sensitive matters."* On the other hand, you may have disagreed with a policy that is not a secret: *"At my company we always accept returns under any circumstances. If we ask for a reason, it is only for informational purposes. It seems to me that some clients take advantage of this, and I think that's unethical on their part. Still, that is the policy, and that is what I do."*

In many cases, an employer hires a person not just because they can do the immediate job, but also because they have the *potential to be promoted.* One concern is that older people don't have the desire to be promoted. Ironically, if you lack the desire for promotion, the employer may decide against hiring you even for the more basic job. Therefore, you might be asked, "Where do you see yourself professionally in three to five years?" If you are interviewing for a professional level job, answering that you don't know or don't care may put your candidacy in serious trouble. You could respond like this: *"It is difficult to tell you the exact position or title I would like to have in five years. I can tell you that I intend to prove my value to this company. If I do, I anticipate that I will be given more responsibility over time."* On the other hand, let's say you are looking at a new job because you want less stress. You could say something like this: *"I am interested in this company because you are a leader in the industry and are highly respected. I am interested in this job because it will be a great opportunity to use my talents and make a contribution in a less stressful environment than I have been used to. If I do well here, and I intend to, there may be opportunities for some new tasks, but I am not looking for promotion per se."*

You may be asked a question that involves *someone else's age* as a factor. For example: "If you accept this position, your immediate manager is going to be younger than you are. Does that pose any problem for you?" You of course will give an answer something like this: *"I respect my manager's ability and position irrespective of his or her age. I anticipate that I will earn respect in return based on what I contribute."* If true, you could add, *"By the way, I have had two managers in the last ten years who were younger than me. That wasn't a problem for them or for me."*

It is a good idea to realize that age may be an *unspoken* concern and incorporate in your answers facts that will put your prospective employer at ease. For example, if you are asked about a time when you worked on a team, this is a good time to discuss teams that included coworkers or managers younger than you. For instance, you may be asked: "Teamwork is very important at our company. Can you tell me about a time when you worked on a team with people from other departments?" You might respond something like this: *"At my previous employer, before the downsizing, we had both formal and informal teams, and these frequently included people from outside my own department. For example, a few months ago, we had a team to work with the IT people on the implementation of a new system that would link functions like finance,*

contract, and marketing together in the same database so we could
respond more quickly to opportunities as they arose. My role was to
identify the specific functional concerns each area had so that the sys-
tem didn't end up making work life more difficult for anyone. I was
also a good bridge between the more veteran people in the depart-
ments and the relatively younger people in IT."

The sample questions noted above are often called *behavioral*
or *situational* questions because they ask you directly about a specific behavior. This makes sense because past behavior is a good
predictor of future behavior. Your answer should include an *exam-*
ple taken from a *recent* situation.

GIVING EXAMPLES WHEN
ANSWERING QUESTIONS

Declaring that you have a certain skill or characteristic is not
enough. You need to have a good example to back it up. One
approach to developing your examples is to think in terms of
Situation, Action, and Result (S. A. R.). For example, suppose
the question is, **"Describe a time when you were faced with**
problems or stresses at work that tested your coping skills.
What did you do?" Answer: (Situation) "On my last job, we
were faced with an unexpected deluge of orders that had to be
processed by the end of the week. This was stressful because we
have the goal of keeping all our stakeholders happy, internal and
external. It was clear that somebody was going to be upset no
matter how I decided to handle this.

(Action) I prioritized all the orders based on two criteria,
namely, volume of products ordered and the complexity of the

order. (Result) We were able to maximize the amount of product delivered because we had a system to handle it, and we were able to minimize harm to relationships because most stakeholders understood the business necessity behind our two criteria."

Here are three tips for giving good examples:

- **Prepare:** Develop at least two examples demonstrating how you exhibited behaviors and skills you may be asked about. One source to look at is the job description. What skills and characteristics does it call for? Another source is a list of generic characteristics that are frequently asked about even when they are not in the job description: *leadership, conflict resolution, problem solving, honesty, teamwork, decision making, dealing with change, giving and receiving criticism, time management, communication (written and oral), persuasiveness, handling pressure, initiative, and dealing with unpleasant or difficult situations.*

- **Clarify:** Before your response, you can ask to clarify the subject or intent of the question. After your response, if you are not sure that you addressed the question, ask, *"Did my example address your question?"* or *"Would you like another example?"*

- **Don't fudge:** Don't make things up, and don't say things that you are not comfortable saying. For example, if you are asked about leadership and feel that you have not shown "leadership," you could say: *"Actually, I see myself as more of a facilitator and team player. I earn respect and get things accomplished by listening, suggesting, and encouraging."*

Your Attitude

Your attitude is going to show itself, so be mindful of some basics:

Nervous Is OK

Looking for a job can be stressful for the job seeker. It can be frustrating just to obtain a job interview, and even then you are going to be judged by complete strangers. Both your pride and your wallet may be on the line. Being nervous is understandable. You don't have to hide the fact that you are nervous. In fact, when your interviewer asks you, "How are you today?" you can answer, "Actually, I am a bit nervous because I really want this job. But I am glad to be here. How are *you* today?" Once you have mentioned your nervousness, you won't have any reason to waste your energy trying to hide it.

The Sun Will Rise Tomorrow

America is full of opportunity. As much as you may want a specific job, your life doesn't really depend on it. If this job interview does not lead to a job, there will be other opportunities if you continue to seek them.

Interviewing Is Also Difficult for Potential Employers

After all, hiring someone is a major investment for the company. Hiring the wrong person will cost time, energy, and money. Passing over the right person will mean losing the value-added benefits the position is intended to produce. Hiring decisions are among the most important a manager has to make.

Be Courteous and Respectful to Everyone

This includes receptionists and others who may appear to be out of the interview circle. Anything you do may be observed, and anyone you have met may be asked for an opinion about you. Make sure that you show professional respect for your interviewer even if she or he is younger than you and/or holds a position less prestigious than you are seeking.

Communicate a Positive Attitude

If you are upset about being back in the job market, leave that mind-set at home. Remember that some employers will suspect that the older applicant is just looking for a paycheck or for something to do. The employer may also be concerned that older employees won't be as engaged or energetic on the job. Your attitude can dispel those concerns. Here is what you can do:

- Reinforce your positive attitude before the interview. Make a list of the things you have accomplished and the skills you have. Before you can convince an interviewer, you may need to remind yourself.
- Be enthusiastic. Playing hard to get is counterproductive.
- Inject energy and vitality into your voice.
- Ask questions that reflect your interest in doing the job well and in the future of the company.
- End the interview by asking about the next step. You might say, *"I am very interested in this position. What is our next step?"*

Be Knowledgeable but Not Dogmatic

One of the concerns about older people is that they tend to be set in their ways. You may be asked about your work style, the type of work environment you prefer, and what kind of people you prefer as coworkers. If you do in fact have immutable principles on these matters, don't be afraid to say so. If your operating principles conflict with those of the company, you won't be offered the job, saving both parties from a bad match. On the other hand, if you have personal preferences, you should let the interviewer know about your flexibility. In this regard, don't confuse principles with preferences:

Principles	Preferences
Honesty	Bluntness; circumspection
Doing a good job	Workaholic; balanced life
Timeliness	Immediately; before deadline
Courtesy	Formality; informality
Protecting proprietary information	Discussing or avoiding certain subjects

Dealing with an Unjust Dismissal

Leave your anger at home. One way to do this is to pour out your wrath on paper. Write everything you would want to say about your unhappy experience, and then print two copies. Crumple one and toss it away. Save the second copy. Rewrite it in a brief, business-like manner. The general theme would be that you had many good experiences, many wonderful friends, and colleagues. Unfortunately, there were problems with a specific individual that just couldn't be resolved. Read the revised text to yourself and use it as a basis for your answer if your unhappy experience is raised at your interview.

Age-Related Concerns

There may be some concerns about your age, even if they are not expressed. It is unfair to everyone involved for you to get hostile

WHAT SHOULD YOU DO IF THEY ASK YOU ABOUT MONEY?

In most cases, answering the interviewer's questions about compensation before you have the job offer is not to your advantage. If you are asked, "How much do you expect to get paid?" any specific number you give is likely to work against you. Your stated number may be too high (unrealistic; out of our range) or too low (no self confidence; may be used against your interests at a salary negotiation). Here is what you should do.

- **Focusing on the right job, not the money:** You could respond something like this: *"What I am interested in most is finding the right job with the right company. I am sure that your compensation package is competitive with the market. If you decide to offer me this position, and I hope you do, I am sure that we can reach an agreement on compensation that makes everybody happy."* If you are interviewing for a part-time or hourly position, you would speak about competitive wage rather than salary.

- **Salary range:** Try not to give a specific number but answer with a salary range that you know is reasonable: *"I haven't thought about this in detail yet, but a salary range between the mid- $60s and mid- $70s seems to be about right."* The bottom of your range should be the absolute minimum you would accept.

- **Interviewer persistency:** Sometimes an interviewer will come at you again after you have given one of the answers

(continued)

above. In that case you could respond, *"I am sure that your compensation package is a good one. What are you planning to offer your best candidate?"*

- **Wage instead of salary:** Let's assume that you are applying for a position in a retail store. You will probably be offered an hourly wage, not a salary. But the general principle applies. Just substitute "wage" for "compensation package" or "salary."

---

about them. Every job seeker faces concerns that must be addressed. If age is one of them in your case, you can overcome it.

Every hiring manager has developed some screening criteria to help identify people they think are the best candidates for the job. Unfortunately, there may also be attitudes or stereotypes that work against older people. That doesn't, in itself, make the interviewer or hiring manager an ageist bigot. However, it does mean that you will have to know what those attitudes and stereotypes are in order to overcome them.

Here are some common, if unspoken, concerns and how you can overcome them:

Overpriced

Paying $10 for a stick of gum is exorbitant. Paying $10 for a steak dinner is a bargain. Price can only be evaluated in the context of value received. You are overpriced only if you are expecting to be paid more than what the best candidate for that job is worth to the employer.

You need to do some thinking in advance of your interview. What are your salary (or wage) expectations and what is your basis for it? You *should not* expect to be paid a certain amount simply because you made that kind of money on a previous job. No employer would owe that to you. On the other hand, you *should* expect to be paid what the job is worth.

Perhaps you are not expecting your previous salary because the potential new job is less stressful, demands fewer hours, or is not related to your previous experience. If that is the case, it is to your advantage to let that fact be known. If you are expecting a salary commensurate with your work history, you should let that fact be known as well. But your expectation must be based on your value to the next employer, not your salary from your last one.

Take a moment to think about this from an employer's perspective. Economists refer to "location-specific human capital." Because of your experience with a specific employer you have gained connections with clients, suppliers, colleagues, etc., and an institutional memory. These have an economic value that may be reflected in your salary. If you leave your current employer, that location-specific value is lost.

The bottom line is this: you should expect a salary that reflects the value added you bring to your next job. A future employer may ask about your salary history. However, your next salary will not be determined by a previous salary, personal pride, or financial need.

Resistant to Change

It may be true that you can't teach an old dog new tricks, but you are not a dog. What you need to do is to prepare examples of changes you accepted or even initiated in the recent past. You can then include some of those examples in your résumé and/or introduce them during the course of your interview.

Examples: (For résumé) *Initiated new order processing system that resulted in a 10 percent reduction in excess inventory.* (For interview) *About 18 months ago, I initiated a new order processing system to alleviate our excess inventory problem. After speaking with people in shipping, warehousing, purchasing, and IT, I developed a plan that took advantage of some new computer capability we were using in other areas. The result was a 10 percent reduction in excess inventory.*

There is a big difference between *resistance to* change and asking questions about a proposed change. For example, if you are asked if you have ever opposed a change, you could answer something like this (if it is true): *"Change is necessary and continuous. On the other hand, we shouldn't confuse change with progress. Simply changing something doesn't automatically make things better. Last year, when a change in our approach to delinquent accounts was suggested, I asked how the change would yield an improvement. I also asked if there was any downside risk. Someone else then asked about transition costs. I like to exercise my professional judgment and not just jump on a bandwagon. Of course, once a policy is instituted, I get behind it 100 percent."*

Can't Work with Younger Managers

If this were true, it would be a serious problem for everyone concerned. It is your job to let the potential employer know that it is not true about you. Prepare examples of your working with younger people. Speak in a tone that reflects respect if they are peers and earned deference if they are managers. *"One of the things I like about my current (or previous) job is that we work with people of many age groups, both genders, and a variety of ethnic identities."*

Won't Put in Long Hours or Will Be Less Productive

This is the concern that you have lost your ambition, lack energy, and/or have come to work because you don't like the senior citizens' center all that much. What you need to do is to work in phrases like *"Let me tell you about my work style. I work to get the job done, and done well, not to leave at 5 p.m. Any job I would be interested in doing would probably require extended hours, at least sometimes." "My last annual review noted that I am one of the most productive employees in the unit. The reason is that I combine dedication, energy, and good judgment."*

The Upside of Age

There is no need to be defensive about your age. Instead you can identify areas where age may be perceived *as an asset* and show that they apply to you.

Perspective and Judgment (Trump Youth and Inexperience)

Good judgment is worth its weight in gold. Further, judgment takes time to develop. Over the years, you have developed the sound judgment that gets things done efficiently and effectively. Your next employer will reap the harvest of what you sowed when you worked for previous employers. Of course, you will need some examples to prove it. *"Last year, when we were considering the implementation of a new computer system, I suggested that we back up vital documents for use during the transition period."*

Asset, Not a Threat

The idea that older folks lose their ambition can be turned to your advantage: Your manager gets the advantage of your talent without the threat that you will go after his or her job. If in fact your goal is to have a good job and do it well, you could say something like this:

"I enjoy what I do, the challenge, the satisfaction, and the people I work with. On the other hand, I have achieved what I set out to do in my career. More promotions are not on my agenda."

Un-Job Hopper

You offer stability. This job would not be simply a stepping-stone.

"For me, this job would be an opportunity to contribute my experience and skills to the success of a new organization. I do not view it as a rung on a ladder or an interim assignment to get my ticket punched."

Role Model for Younger Workers

Your age is also an advantage when you use your experience to help younger people in the company.

"I have a strong work ethic and exercise sound judgment. I know that role model is not written in the job description, but that is one of the contributions I can make, nonetheless."

Ending Your Interview

At some point the interviewer is going to let you know that the interview time is just about over. It is important that you end the interview correctly:

Interviewer: John, I have enjoyed speaking with you today. However, it seems that our time is up.

John: I have enjoyed speaking with you as well. I am very interested in this job. What is our next step?

Notice that John demonstrates two things with his question. *First,* he shows an interest in the job. If John shook hands with the interviewer and looked him or her in the eye while saying this, his stated

A NOTE ON HOW TO DRESS

We are not going to say much about what to wear to your job interview. Unless the employer has given a specific dress code to the contrary, you should dress professionally (A suit and tie for men; a nice modest dress or a nice blouse and skirt for women). Your goal is not to look like a 30 year old if you are a 60 year old. On the other hand, you don't want to seem like a person who hasn't purchased business clothing since the Nixon Administration either. Your personal grooming can be very important. Watch out for hairs protruding from your ears and nose or nails that haven't been tended to lately. Some people recommend dyeing white hair. I do not. If someone is interested in your age, they will find out. Why should you put yourself through the experience of pretending to be someone you are not?

interest will be especially credible. *Second*, John has shown that he has good business sense. An interview is like a business meeting, and every business meeting should end with a "deliverable," namely a clear statement of the next step. By the way, the interviewer may give John a rather generalized or nondescript response. That is OK. John has already made his point.

Follow-Up

After your interview, go to a quiet place and take notes on what transpired. What were you asked? Which of your answers elicited a follow-up question? Did any question make you uncomfortable? That information will help you prepare for your next interview, whether with that company or with another.

Also make notes as to what you need to do next. For example, have you been asked to supply a list of references or a proof of graduation? If so, that's good news. However, you need to make sure to do it sooner rather than later.

Yes, you should send a thank-you note to the person who interviewed you. If three people interviewed you, send a note to each one. There are two reasons:

- Courtesy doesn't go out of season.
- It may help you get the job. Your thank-you note is an indication of sincere interest, which is frequently one consideration for an employer in making a job offer. Also, your thank-you note shows good business sense, and that can't hurt either.

I would send a thank-you note by e-mail as soon as possible and also send a short hardcopy note through the U.S. mail.

A week or 10 days after your interview, I would call the interviewer to express continued interest and to ask if there have been any developments. If you hear some good news from the interviewer, that's great—but don't expect it. Your purpose is to stay in touch. After the first call, you can call again in two weeks or so. If you call more frequently than that, you will be considered a pest rather than a candidate for hire.

An exception would be this: if you receive a job offer from Green Company, you could call your interviewer at Red Company. Ask him or her when you might expect to hear whether or not a job offer will be extended, explaining that you need to respond to another company in the near future.

Once You Have a Job Offer

Corona has been offered a position with Dollar Data. After several months of looking, she was delighted to have the chance to work again. However, Corona was interested in making more money than the offer letter indicated. Here are the four steps I recommend for asking for a higher salary:

- Don't be afraid to ask. If you ask in the right way, the worst that can happen is that the company will say no. (Even then, at least you asked. How would you feel if you didn't ask, and subsequently you find out that you could have made more money?)
- Ask for a higher starting salary only when all other issues are settled. You should be ready to say something like, "I really want this job. My only hesitation is the salary. Although it is a substantial amount of money, I really expected a bit more. If you can increase your salary offer to $50,000 (or whatever amount), I will accept this offer right now." Said that way, you are assuring the company that the only item standing in the way of your acceptance is money and that if they do indeed increase their offer, you will not raise further demands or objections.
- Try to discuss salary face-to-face with your potential employer, rather than on the telephone. On the other hand, use the telephone if a face-to-face meeting is impractical.
- Have solid business reasons for the company to increase its salary offer to you. Do not whine or focus on your personal needs. Here are some examples of good business reasons: (1) you have a higher offer from another company—your potential employer probably doesn't want to lose a good candidate because of uncompetitive salaries; (2) data from your local professional association or your profession's trade journal indicates that a higher salary is warranted; (3) you indicate that you bring more to the job than the description calls for so you are a better catch than the company anticipated.

When you do speak with your potential employer, keep three things in mind:

- It is not pushy, rude, or impolite to seek an improved compensation package.
- Asking for more shouldn't cost you the offer if you ask in the right way. Do not threaten. The right tone is, "If you raise the salary offer to about $55,000, I will accept right now," not "I will take this job only if you offer me more money."
- Be prepared if the answer is "no." Keep your perspective. You were discussing money, not love. The word "no" is not an attack on your self-worth. Also, if you are prepared for a "no," you will have a constructive response ready. For example: *"I am disappointed about the company's position on my salary request. If you had said 'yes,' I would have said 'yes' on the spot. But I understand that there are constraints. I am still interested in this job and in this company. I will let you know if I can accept your offer within a week."*

Now that you have that great next job, let's look in the next chapter at things to remember about life on the job. There may be many adjustments that you have to make, and some myths that you would be better off debunking.

10

Life on the Job: The New Kid on the Block Has Gray Hair

THERE YOU are starting your new job in your 50s, 60s, or 70s. It is important to keep in mind that a job is still a job, and people are still people. You just happen to be older than you used to be (and probably older than many of your coworkers).

Part of starting any new job is doing your part to make the new situation work out. Remember, that you are the new kid on the block and that you will have to adjust to the new neighborhood if you want to be successful there.

Here are some tips that will help you succeed when the curtain goes up:

- **Be ready to act, not to take a bow:** It is easy to feel that you have already proven yourself over a period of years, and you probably have. But the paycheck you get now is based on the work you do *now*. Furthermore, on a new job, you will be working with people who may not have known you way back when. They have no memory of your wonderful track record.

- **Don't ask about your staff or office:** If you are downshifting your work responsibilities, you will probably experience a downgrading in perks as well. You may have realized that fact intellectually, but you need to prepare emotionally as well.

- **Interact with younger colleagues:** Your boss may be the age of your adult children and his or her staff may approximate the age of your grandchildren. Everyone deserves respect, but no one is owed deference based simply on age. You will need to work in an environment where you interact as an equal (or even subordinate) to someone who is younger.

- **Distinguish work from family:** As much as you may enjoy the company of your colleagues and as much as the work-place may "feel like family," be careful to keep in mind that work is really distinct from family. Especially when two or three generations are working together, you want to be careful not to reenact family or parent/child relationships.

- **Update yourself on the company, current events, and the local buzz:** This would be good advice for anyone starting a new job. It is especially important for older workers. Fairly or not, many people will assume that you are uncommitted and simply out of touch with the company's business unless you prove otherwise.

- **Don't replay "the good old days":** It is fine to draw on your wealth of experience to ask constructive questions or to suggest possible solutions. It is not to your advantage to express your ideas in terms of "How we did it in the good old days."

- **Understand part-time, full-time, and overtime:** If you are a part-timer, don't expect to have as much weight in decision making as the full-timers. If you downshifted to have less responsibility and stress, don't expect to get the most interesting assignments. Expect some tension when other employees are working overtime, and your arrangement is that you go home at 5 p.m.

■ **Be aware but don't pretend:** If you worked in a place where people talked frequently about the Minnesota Twins, it would make sense to become conversant with that subject. However, it would not make sense to make believe that you are an ardent Twins fan. You would succeed only in making yourself look foolish and phony in the eyes of others. Similarly, you should be aware of the cultural interests of your coworkers, without making believe that you share those interests if you really don't.

■ **Initiate learning new technology or tackling new challenges:** You benefit from the challenge and the growth. Therefore you will be a more valuable (and more secure) employee. You will also be negating the stereotype that older workers are adverse to innovation, afraid of technology, and not interested in challenge. You may need to overcome your concerns about not learning as quickly as other employees or not getting it right the first time. Staying current is part of the job; walking on water is not.

■ **Be sensitive of safety:** This is especially important for older workers. There is a common perception (not completely without foundation) that you may be more of a risk for a workplace accident. Depending on the work site, check out places where you might trip, knock things over, or break something.

Let's take a look at some myths that can stand in your way.

Some Myths You Can Live Better Without

Try to avoid these mind-sets that may jeopardize your reentry into the workplace.

- **I am going to be better by looking younger:** It is important to be well dressed, so you don't look out of date or out of touch. But youth *per se* is not the issue. A style that is appropriate for a 25-year-old may look ridiculous on you. Similarly, I recommend that you be well-groomed and be especially mindful of visible hair in your ears or nose. However, I don't recommend dyeing your hair. People will know approximately how old you are anyway, so it's unnecessary to go through a daily pretense.

- **I don't have to keep up-to-date as I'm experienced:** While experience is valuable, what really counts is how you apply it to new situations. If your experience helps you exercise better judgment, that is a plus, not a trump card all by itself.

- **I am what I did:** Even if you accept the proposition that "work defines the person," you still need to get your time frame straight. People may respect you for your past achievements, especially if they were aware of them at the time. However, what you do today is a matter for the present tense. Professionally, you are what you *do*.

- **I have worked hard for years so I am owed:** If you stay with the same employer, there may be some sense of loyalty based on past service. However, don't view that loyalty as an open-ended debt. After all, you did get paid all those years. If you are with a new employer, they owe you for what you produce now and nothing more.

Let's take a look at some folks in their 70s and their life on the job.

New Jobs Can Bring a New Sense of Joy

For 50 years, Dean Korn of Carthage, Missouri, worked as a black-smith and in construction. Pick almost any Monday at 7 a.m. and you will find Dean at the local Wal-Mart. However, Dean is a bit different from many other 86-year-olds. He is not an early shopper. Instead he is a full-time employee and will be working at Wal-Mart until 4 p.m., five days a week.

Dean started at Wal-Mart 16 years ago as a favor to his friend, Wally. "Wally had a bad knee, so I asked him how I could help out. Wally was afraid that somebody might replace him permanently if he left, so I just arranged to pitch in while Wally had his knee taken care of. Well, one day I was about to leave, and the manager asked me where I was going. 'Home', I said. 'Well hang on there, I would like you to work here full-time,' he replied. 'What about Wally, when he comes back', I asked. 'Don't you worry about Wally. He can have a job here as long as he wants it,' the manager said. So that's how I got started."

There is a good deal of variety in Dean's job. If one of the managers needs something assembled, Dean is the man. When items need to be transferred from one store to another, Dean loads up his trailer and drives off to Joplin or another nearby city. The job is not monotonous and is considerably easier than the construction job he had when he was younger. Dean enjoys the people who come into the store, many of whom are friends from around town. He has also made some new friends among his coworkers. The paycheck doesn't hurt either.

Dean does have some regrets. He has less time to spend on his hobby, model railroads. More profoundly, Dean told me that, "I wish that I had started at Wal-Mart 20 years earlier. There is enormous potential at Wal-Mart, and you can do almost anything that interests you. They also treat you right. I get four weeks paid vacation and holidays with pay. It took me 50 years of work before I got to Wal-Mart, and I plan to be here for years to come."

Being Needed and Involved

"Hanging around is just not comfortable. Besides, my clients need me." That's how long-time, and very successful, stockbroker Mike Chase explains why he is still working. Family precedent may also be a factor. Mike's father and his grandparents worked until they passed from this earth.

There are other factors. Mike used to enjoy golf, but it just isn't so interesting any more. "I used to enjoy the companionship, but now my friends are all gone. Playing with the younger guys isn't as meaningful, even if they are willing to pick up a game with an older guy like me." Mike doesn't have any other compelling hobbies or interests that overshadow his interest in working.

Mike could take things easier, perhaps downshift by working as a knowledgeable advisor to a younger broker. Instead, he is the first one in and the last one out of the office. "My clients have been with me for years, and that's why I need to do right by them," he explained. "My health is reasonably good, so I am able to work. Not all the people I know are so fortunate."

The brokerage industry has changed dramatically since Mike began over 50 years ago, and he has had to change with it. "Once you read the Wall Street Journal before you entered the office, and that was your main source of daily information. Today, you and everybody else have multiple sources streaming and screaming all day long. The computer, of course, wasn't a factor. Share volume of 400,000 shares per day was a lot. Today a billion shares traded is nothing to note. Products have changed, too. We didn't use to advise clients on mutual funds and derivatives, for example."

Jobs Can Be a Gift of God

"God must have created this job for me," 75-year old Jerry Sonosky exclaimed. Jerry is a customer relations representative in the Pension Benefit Guaranty Corporation (PBGC). As Jerry explains it, "PBGC is a federal agency that deals with pension security issues. People with pension problems call in from all over the country. We help by answering their questions and concerns." The calls are full of pathos and sadness. Death, loss of income, and stress about the status of a pension from a company the caller worked for many years that has now gone bankrupt. "I talk to them one human being to another. Most callers anticipate they will be dealing with a machine, human or electronic. I show them I care and want to help. Oftentimes, I'm older than the caller. That establishes a special connection. Then we can get down to the substance of their concern. Many times I can explain things to them and that relieves at least part of their worries. In the more technical cases, I transfer the call to experts in field offices located throughout the country."

So why is this job like a gift from God? For one thing, Jerry enjoys talking. He practiced law for 40 years and describes himself as a communicator and problem solver, things he says he's always been. "I was a high school and college debater and went to college and law school to become a public policy lawyer so I could help people. A lawyer is someone who knows how to ask the right question and resolve questions and conflicts. I was a staff assistant to a congressperson helping constituents with their problems. Later I was counsel to a Senate committee where I worked on drug and auto safety and environmental laws. After that I was in private law practice for 20 years." The other reason Jerry works is purely pragmatic. He has a sit down job now; a necessity since standing on his feet for prolonged periods is difficult.

Jerry has had other "postretirement" jobs. In 1997, he went to work in the U.S. Holocaust Museum bookstore. "I loved selling and customer relations. In addition, there was opportunity for growth. When I wasn't selling books, I was reading them. Then I went to work in a toy store that specialized in developmental toys. It was fun and meaningful at the same time. I got to be the grandfather figure to a lot of little kids. However, stand-up retail is rough. That's why finding PBGC with the help of the County Senior Employment Resources agency was a godsend."

Why does Jerry work at all? "One reason is that I can't just sit around, although I do have hobbies. The other thing is that while I've made a lot of money, I've also spent a lot of money. So now I need the supplemental income. What would I do if let's say, I won the lottery tomorrow? I'd make certain my wife of 47 years had nothing to worry about if something should happen to me. I would set up a fund so my four grown children and grandkids would be secure. I'd get me a new red Mustang convertible with a white rag-top to replace the 1986 model I now drive. Then, I'd go back to work at PBGC. It's a great place to work and help people at the same time."

The first 10 chapters of this book have been about working. Chapter 11 is about your financial future.

11

Planning for a More
Financially Secure Future

THE BABY BOOMER'S *Guide to the New Workplace* is mostly about working past the age of 55. Employment security until you decide to stop working is, among other considerations, an important part of financial security. However, you will still need to have a source of income when you stop working. This chapter will tell you the basic things you need to know about financial reality so you can be better prepared and more secure.

The good news is this: with proper planning and informed decision making, it is possible to have a financially secure retirement. There is some bad news: it may not be easy and events beyond your control may disrupt the best-laid plans. I am grateful to Greg Winsper, senior vice president, and his colleagues at AXA Financial (www.axaonline.com) for sharing their expertise in financial planning with me.

Determining Income Needs at Retirement

There is no simple answer. A rule-of-thumb number often cited in the popular press is 70 to 80 percent of your preretirement annual income. That range is reasonable if you own a home mortgage free, your children are grown and out of the house, and your lifestyle expectations are moderate. After all, you will no longer have the expenses associated with raising children and going to work. Now consider that many baby boomers are free spenders. Their plans for retirement include doing many (if not all) of the things they dreamed of and deferred during their working years. For them, the percentage might be 100 percent (or even more). So what you will need depends mightily on how you plan to live. If you are planning an upscale, multicar, active, travel-filled retirement you will need more than the person who plans to stay close to home and lives modestly.

There are possible events we should take into consideration that make planning more complicated. For example, we all know when we were born, but none of us know when we will die. With many people retiring early and living longer, you might spend 15, 20, 30 or more years in retirement. (For some people, the number of years in retirement may approximate the number of years they worked full-time.) Will your income sources make upward adjustments to account for inflation? To the extent that the answer is "no" you will be losing purchasing power every year. There are also many unforeseeable, uncontrollable events that could complicate your finances. For example, there is the possibility that you may have an aged parent come live with you, an adult child return home for an extended period, or a spouse become seriously ill. You may lose a job that is paying you well and have difficulty obtaining something comparable. Keeping those things in mind, let's take a look at some key considerations.

When to Start Saving for Retirement

In principle, it is never too early to begin saving for retirement. In practice, many people don't make retirement planning a top priority. That is understandable. There is a mortgage to pay, children to raise, and education bills. The needs that are closer tend to get the focus first. Unfortunately, people who start saving later are in a relatively difficult position. Let's take the hypothetical case of a Steve and Martha Smith, who are both 45 years old. Let's start with the simplifying assumption that the Smiths have saved nothing for retirement. If Steve and Martha want to retire in five years, there is no real way to accumulate a sufficient amount of savings. If we extend their horizon to 10 years, the situation would still be difficult. They couldn't save enough with fixed income securities and equities (e.g., common stocks) would be too risky. If Steve and Martha are thinking of retirement in 15 years, they are in relatively better shape, but it still wouldn't be easy. In fact, even if their time horizon is 20 more years of working prior to retirement, they may need to do some belt tightening. Let's take a closer look.

On one hand, with a 20-year time horizon, the Smiths could invest in equities (which historically have tended to have a higher yield than fixed-income investments. Of course, historical results are no guarantee of future performance). On the other hand, consider how much they would have to save every year they continue to work: for ease of arithmetic, let's assume that Steve and Martha jointly earn $100,000 a year. If they plan on needing 75 percent of their current income in retirement, and if they anticipate living only 10 years as retirees (i.e., they both plan to die on their 75th birthday), Steve and Martha would need to save $750,000 in constant dollars by the time they stop working. If we assume a 6 percent compound return annually, Steve and Martha would need to save $20,388 every year. That is a full 20 percent of their current gross, pretax income. If the timeline for the Smiths was 25 years, they would need to save less every year; if the timeline was 15 years, they would need to save more. Of course, Steve and Martha probably have saved something—and at least one of them is likely to be eligible for Social Security and one or both may well have a pension plan from their employment. Those sources of revenue would mean that the Smiths wouldn't need to save the $20,000 plus we calculated. Also, it is reasonable to anticipate that Steve and/or Martha will earn a pay increase as time goes by. However, there are also some downside factors that must be considered. Our example does not account for unforeseen events like the loss of a job or a serious illness. Further, our example assumed a zero rate of inflation. If the actual rate of inflation for the 10 years the Smiths plan to live in retirement is 3.5 percent, they will need about $98,000 per year in the last year of retirement to equal the $70,000 of purchasing power in their first year. What's more, one or both Smiths may live well beyond the age of 75. They don't want to exhaust their funds and then face 5, 10, or 15 years of financial hardship.

Other Potential Sources of Income

Reverse Mortgages: You can think of a reverse mortgage as a loan against your home. You can be paid all at once, in monthly amounts, or at times and in amounts that you choose. You don't have to pay it back as long as you live in that home.

The *advantage* is that you can draw down the equity value of your home. That does provide a flow of income. Furthermore, you don't have to leave your home. Unlike a conventional loan, you don't need to have a certain income to qualify for the loan, and you don't make monthly payments. It should be noted that, in most cases, you must own your home and be at least 62 years of age.

The *disadvantages* are that a reverse mortgage is not a bottom-less well, and it is not free. The amount of money you receive depends on a number of factors, including your age, your home value, and location. There is a cost to the loan: you are implicitly paying interest. Therefore, the greatest cash value of a reverse mortgage would typically go to the oldest borrowers, living in the homes with the highest market value and who are charged the lowest interest rate. Furthermore, because you are receiving money and making no payments, your amount of debt constantly rises (principal plus interest). The amount of debt you accrue reduces the equity remaining in your home at the time of your death or at the time you move from that home. Therefore, any plans you had to bequeath that home to your children may need to be changed.

Annuities: There are different types of annuities and you should be very careful in deciding which type of annuity, if any, makes sense for you. Simply put, an immediate annuity is a "long term financial investment contract." When you buy an immediate annuity, you pay a financial service institution, like an insurance company, a lump sum of money in exchange for a guaranteed flow of income. However the cost of obtaining that guarantee can be considerable. Also, unless your annuity provides for a survivor's benefit (which comes at a cost), your surviving spouse won't have that flow of income if you die. If you choose an immediate annuity, you are probably paying for it with money you have already saved prior to the time you stopped working.

A deferred annuity is a form of saving program. It is an annuity contract that delays payments of income until you elect to receive them. There are two phases. In the savings phase, you as an investor, add money to your account. In the income phase, the plan is converted into an annuity and payments are received. At that point, you may receive payments in a lump sum or in installments. You can also choose to have a survivor's benefit. If you choose a deferred annuity, you are probably still working and saving in anticipation of the day you stop working.

Inheritance: The popular press sometimes talks about a transfer of wealth between the baby boom generation and their parents. You can read figures in the range of $11 trillion. There are two things to keep in mind. First, that $11 trillion is privately held wealth. It won't be divided on a per capita basis. Second, in the specific case of your parents, whatever wealth they have accumulated may be dissipated by expenses they incur over the years to support themselves.

Mistakes to Avoid

There are a number of mistakes in planning for retirement finances that some people make. We have already discussed waiting too long before you begin to save in a serious way. Here are some more.

- **Being too risk averse when you are younger:** Equities tend to yield greater returns over the long haul than fixed income investments. It pays to take that risk when you are younger because you have time to recoup from a down market cycle.

- **Taking a short-term, instead of a long-term, approach to your investments:** People who follow the prevailing trend in the market are liable to sell assets when they are low and then start accumulating assets again when the price goes up. With that approach you may dissipate a good deal of the capital appreciation your investments should yield.

- **Failing to maximize the value of the pension you receive:** You need to make an important decision in consultation with your spouse. When you opt to take your pension, you will probably be asked whether you want to receive a flow of relatively larger monthly checks that will cease with your death or a somewhat smaller check that your surviving spouse will continue to receive. The risk of the first option is leaving your surviving spouse with insufficient income. However, the monthly cost of the second option can be substantial. One way to address this situation is by buying life insurance on yourself with your spouse as the beneficiary. In many cases, the cost of that insurance will be less than the loss to your monthly pension check. Many people also consider purchasing long-term care insurance as a hedge against the huge bills that could result from a sustained period of illness or incapacitation.

- **Overestimating the value of Social Security:** There are a number of common misconceptions. One is that the full retirement age (the age at which you will receive full benefits) is 65. In actuality, the full retirement age is gradually rising. It is 66 or more for those born in or after 1943 and will be 67 for those born in or after 1960. Furthermore, Social Security is not designed to replace all of your preretirement income. Much to the contrary! If you are an average earner, Social Security is intended to replace about 40 percent of preretirement earnings. There is an inverse scale, so that the higher your earnings, the lower the replacement percentage. Also, some of the changes being considered in Washington would reduce the amount of initial Social Security payments by changing the index upon which they are based.

- **Forgetting that women's situation is often different than men's:** Let us count the ways. First, women, on average, live about five years longer than men. That means that a woman's money has to last longer. Second, women often have fewer years in the workforce. That means fewer years to build up savings in a 401(k) or other retirement plan. It might also mean lower Social Security payments upon retirement. Third, women are considerably less likely than men to receive pension income in retirement (30 percent of women compared to 47 percent of men 65 years of age or older). What's more, for those women who do receive a pension, the benefits, on average, are considerably less because women tend to work fewer years outside the home and tend to be paid less than men.

This chapter is not about giving financial advice. However, it should be clear that financial security after your working years will require serious, realistic planning. Your working years can be a joy. Your nonworking years can also be wonderful if you are financially prepared.

Index

About the Author

RICHARD FEIN received both Master of Arts and Master of Business Administration degrees before beginning his impressive career in advising and program management. He is the founding director of the undergraduate placement program at the Isenberg School of Management, University of Massachusetts at Amherst. Fein has written numerous books including *95 Mistakes Job Seekers Make…and How to Avoid Them, 101 Hiring Mistakes Employers Make and How to Avoid Them, 101 Dynamite Questions to Ask at Your Job Interview, 101 Great Jobs and How to Get Them, 111 Dynamite Ways to Ace Your Job Interview,* and *First Job: A New Grad's Guide to Launching Your Business Career.* In addition to this outstanding list of published work, Fein has also been a guest on over 30 television and radio interviews concerning career issues.